SUPER
KIDS

SUMAN AGARWAL

SUPER KIDS

HEALTHY EATING FOR KIDS AND TEENS

EBURY
PRESS

An imprint of Penguin Random House

EBURY PRESS

USA | Canada | UK | Ireland | Australia
New Zealand | India | South Africa | China | Singapore

Ebury Press is part of the Penguin Random House group of companies
whose addresses can be found at global.penguinrandomhouse.com

Published by Penguin Random House India Pvt. Ltd.
4th Floor, Capital Tower 1, MG Road,
Gurugram 122 002, Haryana, India

First published by Random House India 2015

Copyright © Suman Agarwal 2015

All rights reserved

10 9 8 7 6 5 4

The views and opinions expressed in this book are the author's own and the
facts are as reported by her which have been verified to the extent possible,
and the publishers are not in any way liable for the same.

ISBN 9788184005929

Typeset in Palatino Linotype by R. Ajith Kumar

Printed and bound in India by Replika Press Pvt. Ltd.

www.penguin.co.in

To my three babies, Priyanka, Juhi and Komal.
My life is beautiful and meaningful all because of you!

Contents

PART 2: RECIPES

Junkometer

Your ready reckoner for the popular junk foods . . .

Food Item	Calories (kcal)	Fat (gm)	Score (1 point per 20 kcal)	Round-up Score	Score (1 point per 1 gm of fat)
1 brownie sundae	900	55	45.00	45	55
1 McVeggie burger	465	24	23.25	23	24
1 plate *pav bhaji*	437	20	21.85	22	20
1 cup pasta Alfredo	415	17	20.75	21	17
1 *vada pav*	295	20	14.75	15	20
1 *samosa*	325	17	16.25	16	17
1 Chocobar ice cream	287	19	14.35	14	19
1 grilled cheese sandwich	291	16	14.55	14	16
1 packet Maggi	330	11	16.50	16	11
1 plate *sev puri* (6 *puris*)	350	13	17.50	18	13
1 slice of 12" cheese pan pizza (Pizza Hut)	280	9	14.00	14	9

Food Item	Calories (kcal)	Fat (gm)	Score (1 point per 20 kcal)	Round-up Score	Score (1 point per 1 gm of fat)
½ cup *paneer makhani*	273	24	13.65	14	24
¾ cup cheese risotto	267	13	13.35	13	13
1 vegetable frankie	285	12	14.25	14	12
1 cup macaroni and cheese	260	4	13.00	13	4
1 chilli cheese toast	150	21	7.50	8	21
1 cup caramel pudding	357	7	17.85	18	7
1 cake pop	170	9	8.50	9	9
1 packet of Lay's	150	10	7.50	8	10
1 glass of Coke	126	0	6.30	36*	0
Chocopie	120	5	6.00	6	5

*Coke has been given a higher score because of the high content of caffeine and sugar.

The junk food scores have been calculated as per the amount of calories and fat they have. Children should keep their junk consumption as per this meter to not more than 100 per week. For example, in a week one can enjoy: One brownie or pav bhaji with a glass of Coca-Cola, or a pack of Lay's with pizza, or samosa with chilli cheese toast, etc.

Calorie Chart

Food Product	Serving Size	Calories (kcal)	Protein (gm)	Fat (gm)	Carbohydrates (gm)
Cereals					
Kellogg's Chocos	¾ cup	95	2.3	0.1	21
Kellogg's Corn Flakes	¾ cup	93	2.0	0.1	21
Kelloggs's Wheat Flakes	¾ cup	94	3.0	0.0	20
Kellogg's Frosties	¾ cup	103	2.0	3.0	18
Wheat bread (3½" x 3½")	1 slice (25 gm)	87	3.0	0.4	18
White bread (3½" x 3½")	1 slice (20 gm)	50	2.0	0.0	10
Fruits					
Apple	1 medium (145 gm)	50	0.2	0.4	11
Banana	1 medium (65 gm)	75	0.8	0.2	18
Sapota (*chikoo*)	1 large (70 gm)	69	0.0	1.0	15
Custard apple	1 medium	78	1.0	0.0	18

Food Product	Serving Size	Calories (kcal)	Protein (gm)	Fat (gm)	Carbohydrates (gm)
Elaichi banana	1 (35 gm)	41	0.4	0.1	10
Figs, fresh	2 (88 gm)	33	1.1	0.2	7
Guava	1 medium (120 gm)	61	1.1	0.4	13
Grapes	1 cup (140 gm)	97	1.0	0.3	25
Litchi	7	51	1.0	0.0	11
Mango, ripe	1 medium (70 gm)	52	0.4	0.3	12
Orange	1 medium (120 gm)	61	0.2	0.3	14
Papaya, in cubes	1½ cups (175 gm)	56	1.1	0.2	13
Pear	1 medium (150 gm)	78	0.9	0.3	18
Pineapple	100 gm	50	0.5	0.1	13
Pomegranate	½ cup	46	1.0	0.0	10
Strawberry	9 (120 gm)	48	0.8	0.2	11
Watermelon, in cubes	2 cups (150 gm)	24	0.0	0.0	5
Nuts					
Almonds	12 (16 gm)	105	3.3	9.4	2
Cashewnuts	8 (16 gm)	95	3.4	7.5	4
Dates, dried	3 (16 gm)	52	0.0	0.0	13
Pistachios, roasted	22 (16 gm)	91	3.3	7.0	4

Food Product	Serving Size	Calories (kcal)	Protein (gm)	Fat (gm)	Carbohydrates (gm)
Raisins, brown	30 (15 gm)	46	0.3	0.0	11
Walnuts	3 whole (15 gm)	103	2.3	9.7	2
Dairy					
Amul Processed Cheese	1 tbsp	35	2.2	2.8	0.2
Britannia Cheese Slices	1 slice (20 gm)	62	3.4	5.0	1
Britannia Cheese Spread	1 tbsp	50	2.0	4.0	0
Britannia Cheese Cubes	1 cube	59	3.0	9.0	1
Britannia Daily Fresh Dahi	100 gm	64	3.7	3.0	6
Cream Cheese	1 tbsp	39	1.0	3.7	0
Danone Dahi	100 gm	68	3.5	3.5	6
Kraft cheese slice	1 slice	60	3.0	4.0	2
Milk, buffalo	100 ml	117	4.0	6.5	5
Milk, cow	100 ml	67	3.2	4.1	4
Paneer (made from cow's milk)	100 gm	378	18.0	25.0	4
Soya milk	100 ml	35	3.2	1.6	2
Fats, Oils and Condiments					
Butter	1 tsp	36	0.0	4.1	0
Peanut butter	1 tsp	32	1.3	2.6	1
Cooking oil (groundnut, sunflower, rice bran, safflower, mustard, coconut, etc.)	1 tsp	36	0.0	4.0	0

Food Product	Serving Size	Calories (kcal)	Protein (gm)	Fat (gm)	Carbohydrates (gm)
Olive oil	1 tsp	35	0.0	4.0	0
Ghee	1 tsp	45	–	5.0	–
Honey	1 tsp	19	0.0	0.0	5
Jaggery	1 tsp	26	0.0	0.0	6
Mayonnaise	1 tsp	33	0.0	3.7	0
Mix fruit jam	1 tbsp	48	0.0	0.0	12
Nutella	1 tbsp	80	1.0	4.7	8.6
Sugar	1 tsp	20	0.0	0.0	5
Eggs					
Egg white	1	15	3.0	0.0	0
Egg yolk	1	65	3.0	6.0	0
Chocolates					
Cadbury 5 Star	1 bar (32 gm)	141	1.2	5.1	23
Chupa Chups lollipop	1	40	0.1	0.1	12
Dairy Milk	1 bar (95 gm)	495	7.5	26.5	57
Cadbury Gems	1 packet (11 gm)	45	1.0	2.0	7
Gummy bears	10	87	0.0	0.0	22
Jolly Rancher lollipop	1 (17 gm)	60	0.0	0.0	16
KitKat	4 fingers (35 gm)	146	2.2	8.2	16
Kinderjoy	1 egg	110	2.0	7.0	10
Mars	1 bar (50 gm)	226	1.9	8.8	35
Marshmallows	4 large (28 gm)	90	1.0	0.0	22
Milky Bar	1 small bar (13 gm)	72	1.0	4.1	8

Food Product	Serving Size	Calories (kcal)	Protein (gm)	Fat (gm)	Carbohydrates (gm)
Perk	1 bar (23 gm)	118	1.0	7.0	15
Snickers	1 bar (32 gm)	163	2.9	8.9	18
Toblerone	1 triangle	132	1.4	7.3	15
Twix	2 fingers (58 gm)	285	3.0	14.0	37
Desserts					
Apple pie	1 slice	280	–	–	–
Brownie with ice cream and chocolate sauce	1	945	–	–	–
Cake pop	1	170	1.0	9.0	22
Cornetto ice cream	1	216	–	–	–
Chocobar ice cream	1	287	3.6	19.3	24
Cheese cake	1 slice	730	–	–	–
Chocochip ice cream (Baskin Robbins)	1 scoop	270	–	–	–
Chocolate mousse	1 cup	559	–	29.3	–
Chocolate pastry	1	310	–	15.0	–
Doughnut, choco-frosted	1	204	–	–	–
Danone Strawberry Yoghurt	100 gm	113	3.2	3.1	18
Gulab jamun	1 medium	193	2.0	8.0	17
Ice cream sandwich	1	143	2.6	5.6	22
Macaroons (2")	2 medium	217	1.2	9.8	32
Magnum ice cream	1	260	3.4	15.5	27

Food Product	Serving Size	Calories (kcal)	Protein (gm)	Fat (gm)	Carbohydrates (gm)
Mango Duet ice cream	1	100	0.0	0.0	24
Mini cupcakes with frosting	1	52	0.4	1.6	9
Muffin	1	450	–	–	–
Oreo McFlurry	1	560	14.0	16.0	88
Nestle flavoured yoghurt	100 gm	90	3.5	1.5	16
Rasgulla	1 medium	152	–	–	–
TGI Friday's Brownie Sundae	1 serving	960	9.0	55.0	48
Biscuits					
Bourbon	1 biscuit	47	0.6	1.9	7
Britannia Nutrichoice 5 Grain	1 biscuit	84	2.0	4.0	12
Cream crackers	1 biscuit	35	0.8	1.2	5
Digestive Marie biscuit	1 biscuit	21	0.0	0.0	4
Good Day	1 biscuit	44	0.7	2.1	6
Hide & Seek	1 biscuit	19	0.2	0.7	3
Jim Jam	1 biscuit	57	0.7	2.3	8
Little Hearts	1 biscuit	10	0.1	0.4	1
Marie	1 biscuit	24	0.4	0.6	4
McVitie's HobNobs Oatmeal Cookie	1 cookie	43	0.6	1.6	7
Milk Bikis Milk Cream Cookie	1 cookie	55	0.7	2.4	7
Oreo	1 biscuit	53	0.6	2.3	8
Parle-G	1 biscuit	20	0.0	1.0	3
Pickwick	1 biscuit	26	0.4	0.9	4
Pure Magic	1 biscuit	48	0.6	2.3	6

Food Product	Serving Size	Calories (kcal)	Protein (gm)	Fat (gm)	Carbohydrates (gm)
Treat Orange Cream	1 biscuit	54	0.5	2.7	4
Vita Marie	1 biscuit	22	0.4	0.6	4
Chips/Crisps					
Cornittos Sea Salt Flavour Nachos Crisps	100 gm	489	6.8	24.0	60
Cheeselings	1 cup (37 gm)	180	3.0	7.4	25
Lay's (Classic Salted)	1 small packet (27 gm)	150	1.9	9.6	14
Popcorn, salted	1 bowl (12 gm)	55	2.0	6.0	15
Popcorn, caramel	1 bowl	220	2.0	4.0	42
Popcorn, cheese	1 bowl	68	1.0	5.0	5
Pringles (original)	14 pcs (28 gm)	160	1.0	11.0	14
Fast Food					
Chicken McNuggets	4 pcs	194	10.6	11.9	11
Hot dog	1	315	10.0	18.0	30
McDonald's French Fries	Regular	319	4.5	15.5	41
McDonald's McAloo Tikki Burger	1	337	8.2	13.6	46
McDonald's McChicken Burger	1	416	15.3	21.4	41
McDonald's McSpicy Chicken Wrap	1	488	22.0	23.0	48

Food Product	Serving Size	Calories (kcal)	Protein (gm)	Fat (gm)	Carbohydrates (gm)
McDonald's McSpicy Paneer Wrap	1	740	26.0	47.0	53
McDonald's McVeggie Burger	1	465	11.9	23.9	51
Nachos with cheese	1 serving	346	9.0	19.0	37
KFC Popcorn Chicken	1 serving	400	22.0	26.0	18
KFC Potato Wedges	100 gm	260	4.0	13.0	33
KFC Zinger Burger	1	446	24.1	18.5	41
Domino's cheese-burst pizza	6"	422	21.0	22.0	35
Domino's deluxe pizza (12")	1 slice	196	7.0	12.0	16
Domino's garlic bread	1 slice	117	4.7	3.6	16
Domino's pan pizza	6"	598	23.0	28.0	68
Domino's Thin-Crust Margherita (10")	1 slice	160	6.0	3.0	28
Maggi Masala Noodles (1 medium pack)	80 gm	330	7.5	11.0	49
Maggi Vegetable Atta Noodles (1 medium pack)	80 gm	342	8.0	11.0	51
Maggi Vegetable Multigrainz Noodles (1 medium pack)	80 gm	336	8.0	11.0	51

Food Product	Serving Size	Calories (kcal)	Protein (gm)	Fat (gm)	Carbohydrates (gm)
Indian Snacks*					
Bhel puri	1 plate	284	–	–	–
Chicken frankie	1	432	–	–	–
Cheese grilled vegetable sandwich (regular bread)	1	291	–	–	–
Idli	1 big	66	–	–	–
Masala dosa	1	283	–	–	–
Pani puri	1 plate	475	–	–	–
Pav bhaji	1 plate	437	–	–	–
Sada dosa	1	150	–	–	–
Samosa, large	1	325	–	–	–
Sev puri	1 plate	350	–	–	–
Sizzler, veg	1	490	–	–	–
Vada pav	1	295	–	–	–
Veg frankie	1	285	–	–	–
Beverages					
Amul Kool Lassee	1 small tetrapack (200 ml)	158	4.0	4.2	26
Amul Masti Spiced Buttermilk	1 small tetrapack (200 ml)	62	4.0	3.4	4
Bournvita/ Horlicks with milk	200 ml	155	7.2	6.0	18
Coconut water	200 ml	48	3.0	0.0	9
Energy sports drink	200 ml	160	6.0	6.0	11
Gatorade	200 ml	45	0.0	0.0	12

*Values for these have not been provided due to vast difference in values across different recipes and cooking methods.

Food Product	Serving Size	Calories (kcal)	Protein (gm)	Fat (gm)	Carbohydrates (gm)
Lipton Ice Tea, Green Tea	200 ml	64	0.0	0.0	0
Maaza mango juice	200 ml	108	0.0	0.0	27
Slice mango drink	200 ml	126	0.0	0.0	32
Tang Orange	200 ml	97	0	23.0	0
Coconut water	200 ml	48	9	3.0	0
Soft Drinks					
Coke	300 ml	126	0.0	0.0	33
Diet Coke	300 ml	1	0.0	0.0	0
Fanta/Mirinda	300 ml	141	–	–	–
Pepsi	300 ml	131	–	–	–
Sprite	300 ml	144	–	–	35
Juices					
Appy	1 small tetrapack (200 ml)	134	1.0	0.4	33
Frooti	1 small tetrapack (200 ml)	130	0.0	0.0	32
Real Activ, Apple	1 small tetrapack (200 ml)	88	1.0	0.0	22
Real Activ, Orange Carrot	1 small tetrapack (200 ml)	96	0.0	0.0	24
Real, Cranberry	1 small tetrapack (200 ml)	120	0.2	0.0	30
Real, Guava	1 small tetrapack (200 ml)	120	2.0	0.0	30

Food Product	Serving Size	Calories (kcal)	Protein (gm)	Fat (gm)	Carbohydrates (gm)
Real, Mixed Fruit	1 small tetrapack (200 ml)	112	2.0	0.0	26
Real, Orange	1 small tetrapack (200 ml)	112	2.0	0.0	26
Real, Sweet Lime	1 small tetrapack (200 ml)	112	2.0	0.0	28
Tropicana, Apple	1 small tetrapack (200 ml)	94	0.8	0.0	22
Tropicana, Guava Nectar	1 small tetrapack (200 ml)	150	0.0	0.0	36
Tropicana, Mixed Fruit	1 small tetrapack (200 ml)	112	0.0	0.0	27
Tropicana, Orange	1 small tetrapack (200 ml)	100	2.0	0.0	22

Part 1

Food for Thought

Introduction

When you invest in your child's health, you invest in their future.

Nowadays, with our stressful and hectic routines, and kids living away from home as soon as they start college, it has become more crucial than ever to pay close attention to our health and the foods we eat. It's no longer like the olden days when children ate whatever their mothers gave them, and everything the mothers cooked was healthy and organic. With the onslaught of instant noodles, packaged foods, candies and ice cream, kids these days often turn up their noses at home-cooked meals and traditional, healthy dishes.

Today's children are so logical and aware that when they are simply asked to do things without any explanation, or eat something 'because it's healthy', they usually do not follow instructions blindly. They require every concept, every step and every part of nutrition and good health to be explained to them.

I have been a health freak since I was 12. In my

experience, I have found that it is very important to have good knowledge of food. It takes you a long way and keeps you healthy so that you can get maximum output from a day.

This book explores the struggles that parents face to provide the right nutrition to their school- and college-going kids. I have therefore created recipes for junk food with a healthy twist so that children are always excited about meal times!

The book is divided into two parts. The first part is about nutrition, physical activity and issues faced by parents when dealing with their children's dietary habits. The second part is dedicated to carefully chosen, interesting and tasty recipes which parents can follow to make delicious, healthy meals for their kids.

In this new age of fast food, the nutritional scenario has changed. The challenge we face is very different and quite complex. Our kids are bombarded with easy choices all the time. They need to learn to constantly say 'no' to wrong food. The food that our grandmothers and great-grandmothers advised us to eat might not appeal to us any more. But with more than fourteen years' experience in the field of nutrition, I strongly swear by our traditional basic concepts. For example, I truly believe that children should not have tea and coffee, that they should not leave home without having a glass of milk and that evening snacks also should consist of milk. Every evening, children should engage in some physical activity; also, exposure to the sun is important. I believe that we just need to modify kids' diet to reduce certain foods like fried foods, calorie-dense foods such as cakes and chocolates, fast food, etc. to prevent them from becoming overweight and obese. At the same time, we need to include certain foods and vitamins in their daily intake which will help them face the present-day challenges of a highly automated life—packaged foods, junk foods, high levels of pollution in metro cities and increased stress.

Aspects related to junk food—whether to have it at all, how to have it and how to make it healthier—have been discussed in the chapter 'Unjunk the Junk'.

Though there are ways to make junk food healthy, there are nevertheless certain foods and toxins which need to be totally avoided. These hamper proper growth, preventing kids from reaching their optimum height and weight and developing a healthy body. This is explored in the chapter called 'Let's Tackle the Toxins and Anti-Nutrients'.

Further, there are certain foods that parents, kids and young adults need to be aware of as must-haves, especially when a child is growing up (5–18 years old). This is the time when the bones are growing, muscles are developing and there is higher rate of growth than at other ages. At this time, they need more nutritious food in proportion to their body weight as compared to adults. They don't need a high-protein diet as much as a high-energy, protein-sufficient diet. Sufficient carbohydrates are needed so that protein is spared for growth. But excessive carbohydrates will result in weight gain and obesity. There are ways to control and manage obesity which have also been explained in this book.

Before telling kids what not to have, it's important to educate them about the must-have foods for their optimal growth in height and weight, and teach them about smart foods for boosting memory. I have dedicated a chapter called 'Ten Super Foods' to this.

As kids grow older, sleep patterns tend to change in order to meet academic demands and also in response to peer pressure. Many teenagers prefer to study at night and are quite unaware of what to eat and what to avoid as night-time munchies. So there is a chapter on how to handle exam stress and what are the best midnight snacks.

The nutrition talk is incomplete if we do not emphasize on the power of physical activity. For optimal bone density and strong muscle development, it is very important that kids take part in some kind of sport or activity throughout their growing years. This has been spoken about in the chapter called 'The Need for Exercise: The Power of Physical Activity'.

Health cannot be achieved just through the right foods. Children need to be guided when it comes to social media exposure and hours spent on the Internet. Today, people spend more time with their electronic devices than they do with people. Parents have to be very sensitive and careful when addressing this issue, because they too could be unknowingly suffering from the same habit. It is extremely important to keep this 'digital intoxication' in control. If kids are not steered in the right direction, then we are all at risk of losing them to the virtual world, a very unhealthy world.

This book contains the basic nutritional guidelines for kids between 5 and 11 years of age, with another chapter devoted to kids aged between 11 and 18 years. The nutritional needs and growth patterns for these two age groups vary, so they have been addressed separately in the chapter called 'An Overview of Nutritional Needs'.

It is important that parents get a vitamin analysis done to make sure their kids are not suffering from any vitamin deficiencies. This is addressed in the chapter called 'The Mighty Minerals and Vital Vitamins'.

There are common myths that plague parents and kids regarding things like the goodness of milk, the right bread, how much protein to give, which oil to consume, etc. I tackle these in the chapter 'Myth Busters'.

The second part of the book has recipes, which have been carefully chosen so that parents can follow them without difficulty and make the menu for their kids more interesting and healthy.

This part is divided into six sections. The first four sections—Breakfast, Tiffin, Snacks and Dinner—provide a fair idea about a typical day's menu for a child. Then there is the party menu to help you be the most popular mum on the block, and the dessert section which provides low-calorie dessert options.

I enjoy junk food too and feel that it is unfair to take it away completely from kids. So I have proposed a way in which the junk can be 'unjunked' while still tickling the taste buds. I have cooked these dishes several times, trying to better them to get the perfect junk food–nutrition value taste combination. I am sure parents will enjoy making them as much as I have enjoyed creating them, and I can vouch that the kids will love them.

Ten Super Foods: Ensuring Super Brains for Super Kids

uper foods are foods that increase energy levels, build up strength, improve immunity and make kids grow taller, stronger and healthier.

1. MILK AND YOGHURT

Many fad diets these days advise against including milk in your daily intake. On the contrary, milk is extremely important for children as it is full of good nutrients. Milk and dairy products are rich in calcium, phosphorus, magnesium and protein. Milk protein is the sole and most economic source of first-class protein in vegetarian diet that is easily available everywhere. It is known for building stronger teeth and bones, leading to their growth and development. The most absorbable form of calcium among all super foods is found in milk.

Yoghurt acts a probiotic and provides gut-friendly bacteria. Children who suffer from lactose intolerance can switch to yoghurt as their source of protein. Yoghurt has a higher content of calcium than milk: 100 ml milk has 123 mg calcium, whereas 100 ml yoghurt has 150 mg calcium. 'Because milk and other dairy products are primary sources of calcium, children who consume limited amounts of these foods are at risk for poor bone mineralization.'[1]

In metro cities, one can also opt for organic milk to avoid the harmful effects of the adulteration of milk products. According to the Food Safety and Standards Authority of India, 70 per cent of the milk samples tested in 2012 were found to be adulterated. Harmful substances like detergent and starch were found in the samples.[2] In contrast, organic milk is free of all these substances and easily available in supermarkets these days.

Organic milk is milk from cows or buffaloes that have not been injected with artificial chemicals/hormones to produce milk. Nor have they been fed pesticide-laden grass. It has been reported that in order to meet the increasing demand for milk, these animals are injected with oxytocin to produce more milk, but this hormone can adversely affect the hormonal balance in a child's body.

Almond milk too is gaining popularity these days, but it is not a good source of protein and has a negligible amount of calcium. So it should not replace normal milk for growing children.

Milk has equal distribution of all the three macronutrients—carbohydrates (4 per cent), proteins (4 per cent) and fats (3.5 per cent) per 100 ml—which is probably why milk is also called a 'meal in a glass'.

Brain boosters: *Fat is important for brain health. Full-fat*

yoghurt (especially Greek yoghurt) which has the goodness of
proteins and fats helps in keeping the brain cell membrane flexible
and aids in better transmittal of information.

2. EGGS

Eggs are a phenomenal source of high biological value protein. Egg white is rich in vitamins B2, B6 and D, selenium and minerals such zinc, iron and copper. There are only 12–15 calories per egg white, while the egg yolk has more calories (55–60) and fat, and is rich in fat-soluble vitamins A, D, E and K. Egg also contains the carotenoids leutin and zeaxanthin, which are extremely beneficial for the eyes. The yolk contains more calcium, copper, iron, zinc, manganese, phosphorus and selenium than the white. Eggs are a good source of amino acid choline, which helps in brain development.

There is a growing trend among adults to discard the egg yolk with the notion that it has a high calorie and cholesterol content. As per a study conducted by Harvard School of Public Health, egg yolk plays no role in raising cholesterol levels in the body.[3]

During my nutritional practice, I once prescribed boiled egg to a 65-year-old client with borderline cholesterol, Dhruv Kazi, who joined my programme for weight loss. He was recommended one whole boiled egg every day for two months. By the end of those two months, he had lost 5 kg, and his cholesterol levels had dropped from 190 to 177.

For those who do not eat egg, 200 ml of milk will provide the same benefit.

Brain boosters: *Nutrients in egg like choline, omega-3, zinc and leutin help in better concentration.*

3. SALMON

Proteins from salmon are easily digestible and get quickly absorbed into the body. 100 gm salmon has 20 gm protein. It is rich in omega-3 fatty acids, which help in improving mood and cognition. It also contains iron, calcium, selenium, phosphorus and vitamins A and D. But salmon should not be consumed in large amounts as it may contain traces of mercury.

Brain boosters: *Besides salmon, tuna and sardines are also rich in omega-3. According to Bonnie Taub-Dix, RD, 'The more omega-3s we can get to the brain, the better it will function and the better kids will be able to focus.'[4]*

4. NUTS

Nuts are super snacks for your kids.[5] Many Indian families follow the tradition of having soaked almonds early in the morning, a very healthy practice. Nuts have healthy fats. They make for a good option for mid-morning hunger pangs and snack time.

Roasted or salted nuts are easy to carry and can be consumed directly. Mothers must pack a handful of nuts for their kids in their daily tiffin so that kids are discouraged from reaching out for potato chips, cookies and fried packaged foods, which are highly processed and high in calories, sodium and fat.

An Australian study showed that adolescents who consumed nuts regularly had a healthier BMI.[6] When compared to the calories in snacks, nutritionally, nuts are better. Most children's favourite combination of nuts is cashewnuts (good source of zinc and iron), almonds (rich in vitamin E) and pistachios (rich in iron).

Brain boosters: *Vitamin E in nuts prevents cognitive decline as we grow older.*

5. BERRIES

Berries like strawberries, raspberries, blueberries and blackberries are good sources of instant energy. They are great finger food options, especially after a sports activity. They are rich in phytonutrients, antioxidants and folic acid, which help in boosting immunity. They also enhance your child's brain function and dental health.

Berries make for an excellent replacement for sweets and candies. Five strawberries have higher antioxidant levels than three apples and four bananas. Berries are also rich in quercetin, which alleviates allergies like asthma.

Brain boosters: *Antioxidants in blueberries are known to improve learning capacity and locomotor skills.[7]*

6. BANANAS

Contrary to popular belief, bananas are not fattening. In fact, bananas are rich in phosphorus and an excellent source of fibre. A study by Imperial College of London stated that children who ate one banana per day had 34 per cent less chances of developing asthma.[8] Children who are involved in competitive sports like swimming, running, etc. should have a banana for instant energy. They are a perfect hunger fix. High-energy foods like bananas are very beneficial for today's generation plagued by low energy levels and lethargy.

7. CARROTS

Carrots are rich in antioxidants, vitamin A and fibre. They make for handy, on-the-go snacks, being low in calories (one carrot has 30 calories). Carrots help in minimizing dental problems in children. They help in the production of saliva that in turn helps in alkalizing the acid-forming bacteria that are the cause of cavities. Being rich in vitamin A and beta-carotene, carrots improve eyesight and immunity, along with adding a glow to the skin. Raw carrots are used as a home remedy to help in treating worms in children.

8. SPINACH

The beloved cartoon character Popeye has made spinach very popular among kids. Raw or cooked spinach contains twice the amount of vitamin K you need daily. Vitamin K is a fat-soluble vitamin that does not get diminished by cooking or washing. Spinach is also a good source of iron, calcium, potassium, manganese, fibre and vitamins B6 and A. Vitamin K, calcium and magnesium help in maintaining and improving bone health. But spinach also has coenzyme Q10, polyphenols and betaine, which are better absorbed in the body than iron. However, oxalates present in spinach prevent the absorption of iron. Vitamin-C-rich foods like lemonade or chicken cooked with spinach can help in better absorption of iron in food.

9. BEANS AND PULSES

These are rich in iron and protein. The iron content in beans—especially kidney beans and black-eyed beans—helps restore the cognitive function to normal. The inclusion of beans and pulses in one's diet, especially in vegetarian diets, can help in better cognitive function.

10. WHOLE GRAIN

Whole grains have low glycaemic index. Starting the day with whole grain cereal helps children pay more attention in class. Whole grains are complex carbohydrates, that is, they are rich in fibre and are the brain's main source of nutrition. Some examples of whole grains are red millet (*nachni/ragi*), wholewheat (*atta*), oatmeal and sorghum (*jowar*).

Brain boosters: *Fibre ensures that glucose is released slowly so that the brain gets a constant supply of energy.*

Harsh, a teenager, was very active in sports but still overweight. He was suffering from high cholesterol. He came to me with his mother and we balanced his meals with a good amount of soluble fibre, which is present in pulses and oats, and insoluble fibre, which is present in vegetables and fruits. He lost 5 kg in two months with a tremendous drop in body fat which helped in reducing his cholesterol levels. He has been maintaining his weight with us and has been balancing his meals. Since he is a vegetarian, we helped him choose the right dishes whenever he wanted to enjoy cuisines like Italian, Chinese and Continental. To replace the non-vegetarian sources of protein in these cuisines, which are usually chicken and fish, we suggested tofu and stir-fried vegetables and pasta with beans to enhance the protein content of his meals and reduce the carbohydrate content for a complete balance of nutrients.

Let's Tackle the Toxins and Anti-Nutrients

Kids nowadays have easy access to many cuisines and junk food items. It is important for parents to be aware of the toxins present in certain foods so that they can guide their children to choose the right foods and limit the intake of toxic foods by simply being smart about it.

1. CAFFEINE

With the rising popularity of cafes like Café Coffee Day, Barista, Starbucks, Costa Coffee and various other coffee shops, we frequently see many adolescents going to these places 'to chill'. However, excessive caffeine can reduce the uptake of calcium, which is essential for bone accretion and skeletal growth, from meals, especially milk. In my nutritional practice with kids, I have observed that consumption of too much caffeine affects a child's height and weight. I have frequently noticed that kids who regularly drink tea, coffee and colas have under-average height growth per year than the ones who do not drink these caffeinated beverages.

Four cups of tea are equivalent to one cup of coffee. The caffeine content in coffee is 100–150 mg as compared to 15–20 mg in tea. But if your child has thalassaemia minor, then it is better to allow only green tea to him/her. Normal tea is in any case not good for children. High intake of green tea also tends to lower folic acid levels. A study revealed that high level of caffeine consumption may lead to anxiety in children and teenagers.[9] When the caffeine wears off, it aggravates feelings of depression. Aerated drinks like Coca-Cola, Pepsi and Thums Up have high levels of caffeine and sugar. A bottle of Coke and Pepsi has 35 and 38 mg of caffeine, respectively.

Listen to me: *Till the age of eighteen, girls and boys should limit their coffee, tea and cola intake to two cups/glasses a week.*

CAFFEINE CHART

Beverages	Measure	Quantity (ml)	Level of Caffeine (mg)
Tea	1 cup	240	25
Coffee	1 cup	240	Above 75 and as high as 200
Green tea	1 cup	240	25
Red Bull	1 can	250	80
Coca-Cola	1 can	330	35
Herbal tea	1 cup	240	0
Sprite/Fanta	1 can	330	0

Beverages	Amount	Quantity (ml)	Level of Caffeine (mg)
Starbucks Hibiscus Refresher	1 glass	440	45–55
Iced tea	1 cup	240	5–40

2. SWEETENERS

Artificial sweeteners are not good for your child's health. Below are some of the common sweeteners found in junk food, candy, chocolates, chewing gums and such foods which constitute a chunk of what children eat every day.

a. **Sucralose:** This is the main ingredient in Sugar Free, Natura and Splenda. It causes swelling of the liver and kidney and shrinkage of the thymus gland (which helps in the production of T-cells which increase immunity). Artificial sweeteners do not get cleared easily with the normal digestive process; the residues tend to float in the gut.

b. **Aspartame:** It is found in diet cola drinks which are very popular among teenagers. It leads to memory loss and affects brain growth. As per Dr Russell Blaylock, retired professor of neurosurgery at University of Mississippi Medical Center, aspartame is not safe for the growing brains of children, a fact he explains in his book *Excitotoxins: The Taste that Kills*.[10] As per Dr Lenden Smith, MD, paediatrician, it has ninety-two bad health effects.[11]

c. **Maltitol:** It is a major ingredient in sugar-free chocolate, chewing gums and hard candies. It can lead to diarrhoea, excessive gas and flatulence. It is okay to consume in limited amounts.

d. **Sorbitol:** Sorbitol is sugar alcohol. It is present in sugar-free mints. Again, in very small amounts it is okay. But if taken in greater amounts, for example, more than six–eight mints per day, it can lead to cramps, diarrhoea, gas and flatulence.

Listen to me: I have never allowed in my treatment or encouraged children to consume chewing gums that contain artificial sweeteners. Artificial sweeteners like sucralose and aspartame are found in various sugar-free products in the market. Even adults are cautioned against overconsumption of these chemicals. Very popular diet sodas are a total no-no and I tell all my adolescent clients to rather choose regular sodas than diet sodas.

3. HIGH FRUCTOSE CORN SYRUP (HFCS)

HFCS is made from genetically modified corn and is present in ready-to-eat cereals (Rice Crispies, Chocos, Froot Loops), baked goods, cakes and candies. Most American chocolate bars have HFCS. Excessive consumption of foods containing HFCS can lead to arthritis, diabetes, insulin resistance, obesity and heart problems. As per confectionerynews.com, the popular American confectionery brand Hershey's has taken a pledge to not use HFCS and genetically modified ingredients in its Hershey's Kisses and milk chocolates.[12]

Listen to me: Parents must be vigilant about checking chocolate labels for high HFCS content and choosing chocolates very carefully. Encourage kids to replace dessert and chocolates with fruits or frozen fruits like grapes and strawberries. I have included many low-calorie food options in the dessert section of this book which are easy to make, rich in calcium and iron and which could easily satisfy their sweet cravings.

4. MAGGI

This is probably the most popular snack among children. A packet of Maggi has 3.5 gm of salt. I have always maintained that Maggi is not healthy and have never allowed my clients to have it. It was recently banned in India due to its high lead and MSG content. Monosodium glutamate (MSG) is alleged to harm kids' brains and get them addicted to the taste.

Pratik Goyal, executive director, Bajrang Agro Industries, says, 'The process of making instant noodles involves deep frying of the noodle cakes in various kinds of oils, primarily palm oil. The final product after frying contains anywhere from 17 to 20 per cent oil. Due to health reasons, manufacturers outside India are now shifting to the new technology of making instant noodles without frying, but in India this remains the status quo' (Private communication, 20 March 2015).

Noodles like hakka noodles, stick noodles and handmade noodles are dried in ovens and are not fried; hence, they are healthier than fried instant noodles.

Pratik also says, 'Kurkure and potato chips are again deep fried items. They contain anywhere from 30 to 45 per cent oil, usually palm oil or cotton seed oil. Hence, they are not the best items for health if consumed in large quantities. Puffed snacks on the other hand are totally baked and hence have 0 to 5 per cent oil content and can be safely consumed' (Private communication, 20 March 2015).

Listen to me: Strike out Maggi from your grocery list. In fact, go for regular noodles and pasta which are not instant, for bringing in the zing of noodles in your kids' menu, instead of a shortcut like Maggi. Don't be mistaken, the healthier 'atta noodles' are just as bad.

5. FOOD ADDITIVES AND COLOURS

Food colours like Blue 1, Blue 2, Yellow 5 and caramel colouring cause cancer, brain damage and tumours. Hence, it is better to avoid them. A study states that food colouring can lead to attention deficit hyperactive disorder.[13] Here is a list of food additives that can be harmful to children:[14]

a. **Blue 1**: Used in bakery products, candy and soft drinks. Can damage chromosomes and lead to cancer.
b. **Blue 2**: Used in candy and pet food beverages. Can cause brain tumours.
c. **Citrus Red 1**: Sprayed on oranges to make them look ripe. Can damage chromosomes and lead to cancer.
d. **Green 3**: Used in candy and beverages. May cause bladder tumours.
e. **Yellow 5**: Used in desserts, candy and baked goods. May cause kidney tumours.
f. **Yellow 6**: A carcinogen used in sausage, beverages and baked goods. May cause kidney tumours.

g. **Red 3**: A carcinogen that is added to cherry pie filling, ice creams and baked goods. May cause nerve damage and thyroid cancer.

h. **Caramel colouring**: Used in soft drinks, sauces, pastries and breads. When made with ammonia, it can cause cancer in mice. Food companies are not required to disclose details if this ingredient is made with ammonia.

i. **Brown HT**: Used in many packaged foods. Can cause hyperactivity in children, asthma and cancer.

j. **Bixin**: Food colouring that can cause hyperactivity in children and asthma.

k. **Norbixin**: Food colouring that can cause hyperactivity in children and asthma.

l. **Annatto**: Food colouring that can cause hyperactivity in children and asthma.

Most processed foods have certain amounts of colouring and preservatives. They have been linked to having carcinogenic properties and can lead to obesity and insulin resistance.

Listen to me: *It is difficult to stop kids from consuming things like imported chocolate bars, ketchups, packaged and genetically modified wafers, sweetened cereals, candies, carbonated drinks and certain ice creams. But limiting their consumption and making them more aware of the side effects can lead to a better and healthier lifestyle.*

6. FISH

There are certain fish like shark, king mackerel and

swordfish which contain high levels of mercury that can lead to neurological problems like cognitive and motor deficits.[15] Such fish should be consumed in limited amounts, and avoided as far as possible.

7. MICROWAVE POPCORN

These days, most households have a microwave. Microwave popcorn is a very popular snack among kids, but, as per Dr Oz, cardiothoracic surgeon, author and television personality, the popcorn bag is lined with a chemical called diacetyl, a synthetic butter flavouring that is very harmful. Dr Oz explains that the typical smell you get when you make microwavable popcorn is actually that of diacetyl. It was reported that people who worked in the factories manufacturing microwavable popcorn developed a disease called 'popcorn worker's lung' from inhaling diacetyl (see Wikipedia article on Diacetyl, under 'Worker Safety').

The second problem is PFOA, another chemical that lines the bag. Dr Oz says that 20 per cent of this chemical in our bodies comes from microwave popcorn. PFOA can cause thyroid issues, high cholesterol and bladder cancer.[16]

Listen to me: Microwave popcorn should be struck out from your grocery list. It is better to make popcorn the traditional way in a cooker. I even avoid heating food in a microwave due to harmful radiations. I threw out the microwave from my kitchen years ago.

Un-Junk the Junk

Now that we've learned a little about healthy eating, it is time to tackle the actual root of the problem. Junk food is the perpetual bone of contention between parents and kids. It is understandable that kids cannot completely swear off junk food. But there is always a middle ground that both parents and kids can reach about how much junk to consume and when. Parents need to sit with their children and make a list of their favourite junk food. They can then mutually agree on spacing them out through the week so that the child's nutritional needs are not compromised while at the same time the child is also not deprived of his favourite treats. For example, soft drinks could be had on weekends, pizza could be on Wednesday, fried wafers or chips could be every Tuesday evening, pasta could be another day. And maybe chocolates only on Sundays.

Junk foods are called junk because they have high amounts of simple carbohydrates/sugar, sodium and trans-fatty acids or saturated fats. They are low in protein and body-building minerals like calcium and iron.

My previous book, *Unjunked,* also covers more alternative recipes to junk foods.

HOW TO UNJUNK THE BELOW-MENTIONED
JUNK FOODS

Junk Food	Culprit	Recommended Frequency of Eating	Healthier Options
Aloo patty burger	Calories, fat	Once a month	Mini Sliders (p. 186)
Bhujia	Fat, sodium	Avoidable	Nachos Bhel (p. 191)
Chinese bhel	Food colour, fat	Completely avoidable	Nachos Bhel (p. 191)
Chips/ Kurkure	Sodium, additives and preservatives, fat	Avoidable	Kurmura Bhel
Doughnuts	Fat, sugar	Avoidable	Date and Walnut Pops (p. 217)
French fries	Calories, fat, sodium	1 small pack, once a month	Baked Vada Pav (p. 76)
Instant noodles	Sodium, fat, preservatives	Completely avoidable	Spinach and Spaghetti Bake (p. 172)
Ketchup	Food colour, sodium, additives and preservatives	Not more than a tablespoon whenever required	Mint or Tamarind Chutney

Junk Food	Culprit	Recommended Frequency of Eating	Healthier Options
Microwave popcorn	Chemical lining the bag (Diacetyl)	Completely avoidable	Popcorn made in a pressure cooker
Pani puri	Fat, carbo-hydrates	Once a fortnight	Nutri Chaat on Bread (p. 134)
Pav bhaji	Fat, carbo-hydrates, calories	Avoidable	Power-Packed Pav Bhaji (p. 170)
Pizza	Carbo-hydrates, calories	Completely avoidable	Mini Paneer pizza (p. 132)
Potato frankie	Carbo-hydrates, calories	Completely avoidable	Chana Kebab Roll (p. 106), Italian Egg Roll (p. 113)
Samosa	Calories, fat, carbo-hydrates	Completely avoidable	Chhole with Potato Tikki (p. 156)
Soft drinks	Sugar, caffeine, calories	Once a week*	Minty Fruity Cooler (p. 206)
Vada pav	Fat, calories, carbo-hydrates	Once a month	Baked Vada Pav (p. 76)
Veg spring rolls	Calories, fat	Once a month	Sweet and Sour Dragon Roll (p. 123)

*refer to chapter 'Let's Tackle the Toxins and Anti-Nutrients'

Listen to me: Don't banish junk food from your child's diet. Pick and tweak your junk food smartly!

Rima, a tall, broad-built girl, came to me when she was seventeen, with complaints of mild hairfall and obesity — 120 kg is a lot of weight to carry at this age. Her diet analysis was done and I balanced her diet with required amounts of protein, fat and carbohydrate. Foods like *farsaan*, Maggi and *papad* were eliminated and substituted with healthy snack items like *vada pav* toasties, homemade *bhel* without *sev* and *papdi*, etc.

After blood tests, we also came across certain underlying hormonal problems that she was unaware of. Along with the poor diet, hormonal imbalance was another reason for her hairfall and weight gain. We guided her through right doctors to solve the root cause of her weight gain. After following the suggested diet and exercise, Rima lost 28 kg, with phenomenal reduction in her body fat. Along with that, her hormones stabilized to a better range. By the end of the programme, her confidence had increased and she looked happier than ever.

Childhood Obesity

Childhood obesity is now known as the New World's Syndrome. As per a study conducted by the National Diabetes, Obesity and Cholesterol Foundation, in 2010, Mumbai ranked second in childhood obesity. It was found that 30.4 per cent children in private schools and 7.9 per cent in public schools were obese. Dr Motwani, laparoscopic and general surgeon, says that one out of five children in Mumbai is obese or overweight.[17]

Obesity doesn't come alone. It brings along more problems like hypertension, type-2 diabetes, cardiovascular disease, metabolic syndrome, polycystic ovary syndrome (PCOS), low self-esteem and orthopaedic problems.

Let's explore the reasons why obesity has become such a cause of concern in recent times.

- There is an increased demand by parents and teachers on kids to perform in academics and a lot of importance is placed on examination results. Kids have no option but to take extra tuitions to better their academic results which leave them no time for play or to engage in sports activities. Parents as well as academic institutions need to understand that for the overall development of the child, there should be equal thrust on physical activities and studies.

Listen to me: Parents should encourage their child to engage in at least one physical activity every day. It can be anything from sports to dance to swimming or cycling for about thirty to sixty minutes.

- Western fast food joints like McDonald's, KFC, Domino's, Pizza Hut, Subway and Burger King have mushroomed in major cities in India. It is common knowledge that the food available in these joints is highly processed and laden with preservatives, food additives, emulsifiers and stabilizers. They are calorie-dense and fattening too. With decreased physical activity and increased intake of such food items, is it any surprise that we are battling obesity? All this junk has replaced our traditional *upma*, *poha*, *dosa*, *idli* and *bhel* which were better and healthier, non-frozen, fresh snacking options. Even our traditional dinners like *roti*, dal, vegetables and curd have been replaced to a large extent by pizzas, burgers, pasta, Subway sandwiches and french fries, which are usually double in calories, low in fibre and high in saturated fats. It may be difficult to completely avoid fast food joints due to peer pressure and their high appeal to our taste buds, but the consumption should not get out of hand.

Listen to me: Visiting fast food joints should be restricted to not more than once a week.

- With WhatsApp, Twitter, Facebook, Instagram, Snapchat taking over lives, it's hard to find a teenager who isn't stuck to the phone. This does not stop even after dinner and late into the night. I have hardly met any teenager who sleeps before 11 p.m. A child may effectively get only six to seven hours of sleep, but the requirement of the body in order to maintain proper growth and repair functions and brain power is eight to ten hours.[18] Research suggests that children and young adults who get too little sleep tend to weigh more than those who get sufficient sleep. A study published in *Pediatrics* looked at 2,048 racially diverse fourth-graders and seventh-graders who were participating in a study on childhood obesity in Massachusetts. Lack of sleep is considered a risk factor for obesity, so the children were asked how long they slept and if they felt they needed more sleep. They were also asked how often they slept with an iPod, smartphone or cell phone in their bed or next to the bed. 57 per cent said they slept near a small screen.[19]

Listen to me: Certain house rules should be followed for a good night's sleep. Have a heart-to-heart chat with your kid and explain to them the downside of digital intoxication. Encourage your child to disable mobile data from 11 p.m. to 7 a.m. to ensure sound sleep, which will in turn result in better physical and mental growth and prevent weight gain.

- Midnight munching is a common trend and could be one of the major culprits for causing obesity in children. Teenagers who are awake late into the night may indulge in junk foods like chocolate, ice creams, pastries, colas, chips, popcorn, etc., which adds unnecessary calories and saturated fats to the body and leads to obesity.

Listen to me: Midnight munching should be avoided. If the child is studying and feels a pang of hunger, he/she can have finger foods like grapes, berries, carrot sticks, apples and nuts and sip on herbal teas.

- 'Teenagers are vulnerable to unrealistic attitudes regarding the amount of time and effort necessary for effective weight management. Diet fads and drugs appear to provide the quick remedy food they seek.'[20] Obesity management for kids is more serious and should be handled with care, or else fad diets and health plans can become a lifelong story of yo-yo-ing weight loss and gain. Instead of concentrating only on weight loss, as a parent, you should adopt a holistic approach to child obesity. Consult a nutritionist, an endocrinologist and a paediatrician, and provide immense support to your child in battling this issue. There is also need for a careful and sensitive approach to bring behavioural and lifestyle changes in your child. I have observed that hormonal imbalance is often an underlying condition of obesity, so professional guidance is imperative. Many parents keep berating their child, 'You are eating junk, you are not exercising, you are just sitting in front of the TV like a couch potato', but the real culprit may either be insulin resistance or hormonal imbalance.

Listen to me*: I believe in the Hara Hachi Bu principle. Hara Hachi Bu is a Confucian teaching that instructs people to eat until they are 80 per cent full. Simply put, it means you should leave some room in your stomach at the end of every meal. The reason is that it takes the stretch receptors in the stomach about twenty minutes to tell the brain how full you really are. Also, the gastric juices, enzymes and acids take about twenty minutes to reach the stomach. So you will actually feel fuller twenty minutes after you put your fork down. If you eat until you are 100 per cent full, you will go 20 per cent over capacity with every meal and your stomach sac will stretch to accommodate this extra food. We have been traditionally told by our mothers and grandmothers 'pet bhar ke khao'. But this has to change.*

Shristi Goel, a seventeen-year-old student, joined Selfcare on 27 February 2012 with the purpose of achieving weight loss and a healthy lifestyle. She had high blood pressure and no other medical issues, but she thought she could never lose weight. She met our branch head Adity Killa at Selfcare, Kolkata, to modify her lifestyle along with diet, exercise and proper vitamins. Adity and I designed a well-balanced food plan for Shristi and since then she has seen a complete change in her health. Weight loss came with health benefits for her. At Selfcare, weight loss was a stepwise process. Certain problems that she was not aware of and that were affecting her weight loss process were brought to her notice. In the process, certain vitamin deficiencies and hormonal imbalances (insulin resistance and increased prolactin levels) were also taken care of by guiding her to the right doctors. Along with a controlled, well-balanced diet, a simple exercise regime and basic vitamins were also suggested to help her achieve her health goal. Diet was made more interesting by adding a variety of options to make sure that she enjoyed her diet journey and could sustain it for a longer time. After losing 52 kg and 16 per cent fat, she felt more healthy and energetic. Her blood reports showed good results. It took her less than three years to achieve this weight loss. This shows that a healthy weight loss journey may be a lengthy process but it bears good fruit in the long run. You can even reverse your chances of becoming a diabetic in the future. You just need to be patient and determined.

The Need for Exercise: The Power of Physical Activity

In this digitally active, highly automated, social-media-crazy world, physical activity is the key to good health for this generation.

The US Department of Health and Human Services in 2008 recommended that a youth should be active at least sixty minutes each day, including participating in vigorous activity at least thrice a week. In addition, muscle-strengthening and bone-strengthening activities should be included in the sixty minutes of activity at least thrice a week. Activities like swimming, running, football, cycling and skipping should be included in the routine. It has been observed that the muscles which are gained in pubertal adolescent age are not short-lived.

Obesity paves the way for many other chronic diseases for a person. Hence, an equal focus on diet and exercise is required to see results. For a child's well-being, parents tend to focus largely on academics, but the same amount of emphasis should also be given to exercise in order to ensure physical and emotional health.

THE POWER OF PHYSICAL ACTIVITY

1. **Bone health:** Exercises like jogging, trampoline, dancing, skipping and all sports help in improving bone density.
2. **Height gain:** Certain exercises such as swimming, stretching, cycling, basketball and throw-ball aid in height gain.
3. **Muscle strength:** Swimming, push-ups, pull-ups, sit-ups, resistance training, ballet and all the above-mentioned exercises help in building muscle.
4. **Preventing obesity:** Aerobic exercises like cycling, swimming, walking, jogging and sports activities such as basketball, football, tennis, etc. help control and prevent obesity.
5. **Better posture:** Exercises that improve a child's posture are the exercises for the upper back and shoulders, gymnastics, yoga, stretches, dance and ballet.
6. **Exam time:** Walking, cycling, jogging, table tennis, zumba and dancing are good exercises. Even thirty minutes spent in any of these activities will boost energy levels, clear the mind and relieve stress.

Exercising helps in optimizing the brain's function by increasing blood flow to the brain. The blood delivers oxygen and glucose which the brain needs for heightened alertness and mental focus. A study conducted in the Columbia University lab in 2007 revealed that a three-month exercise regime can increase blood flow to the part of the brain responsible for memory and learning by 30 per cent. Studies report that physical exercise decreases anxiety, reduces depression and improves mood and outlook in children. In addition, their quality of sleep is also improved.[21]

As per Mahan et al., the authors of *Food Nutrition and Diet Therapy*, young adolescents are at a higher risk of dehydration because they produce more heat during exercise but have less ability to transfer heat from muscles to the skin. Hence, every physical activity should be accompanied with a high-carbohydrate drink so that the proteins are spared for recovery.[22]

Listen to me: *Besides sports and other types of physical activities, parents should lay emphasis on being active through the day too and encourage their child to make healthy lifestyle choices instead of unhealthy ones.*

Some healthy alternatives to unhealthy choices are the following:

Unhealthy choices → *Healthy alternatives*

Phubbing → *Meet a friend and go for a walk*

Taking escalators → *Take the stairs till the sixth floor*

Ordering the servant to get food → *Get it yourself*

Chilling with a friend at a cafeteria → *Go for swimming or play a sport in a group*

Playing virtual games like FIFA → *Play actual outdoor games like soccer*

FUN FACTS

- Exercise as simple as a fifteen-minute walk can decrease chocolate cravings by a full 12 per cent according to international research journal *Appetite*.
- Exercise helps spike creativity that can be used in simple, everyday tasks and activities as well as in creative endeavours like writing and painting.
- Exercise can improve your self-confidence levels and self-esteem, so you feel good about yourself and naturally smile more.

Ramona, twenty-four years old and a badminton champion, came to us with complaints of knee pain, reduced stamina and low energy levels. After a detailed analysis and understanding of her lifestyle, it became evident that her diet was not well balanced to meet the requirements of a sport activity! Immediately, corrective measures were taken. Being a badminton player, Ramona required more energy compared to her peers who did not engage in sports. Importance of pre-workout and post-workout meals was explained to her. Well-balanced pre- and post-workout meals helped her improve her energy levels during the matches and kept her going through long hours of practice, thereby helping her improve her performance.

Phubbing: A Growing Concern

The American Academy of Pediatrics cautions that children 'need more real face time than screen time, more laps than apps'.

As per the *Collins English Dictionary*, phubbing is the act of snubbing someone in a social setting by looking at your phone instead of paying attention to them.

Till a few years ago, parents were apprehensive and cautious about their kids watching excessive TV. Now, that concern seems small in the face of phubbing or digital intoxication. Today's wired kids are slaves to their phones, laptops and tabs, and are suffering from FOMO (fear of missing out). What they are actually missing out on instead is stability. Today's teenagers are easily agitated, have less patience and suffer from excessive mood swings.

As per the American Academy of Pediatrics (2013) and the Canadian Paediatric Society (2010), children aged five and above should not have more than two hours of daily recreational screen time.[23]

Let's also not forget that due to excessive exposure to these screens, along with psychological problems, children will also certainly face physiological problems such as bad vision, bad posture and obesity.

DIGITAL REHAB

- Children should be told to avoid putting phones in their pockets. Instead, carry a pouch or put it in your bag.
- During exams, encourage them to stay off social networking sites which are more of a distraction and less of a communication channel..
- On the dining table and in restaurants with family or friends, switch off your phone or put it on silent. It is rude to be on your phone when you are with others.
- Charge phones at least 5 feet away from your bedside while sleeping.
- Melatonin, the hormone responsible for inducing sleep, is secreted when surrounding light becomes dim. This is the reason why in earlier days a lot of emphasis was laid on sleeping and waking cycles. It is also the reason for the famous quote by Benjamin Franklin: 'Early to bed and early to rise makes a man healthy, wealthy and wise'. Melatonin secretion is largely disrupted by bright indoor lighting, and light from the computer, tablet, television and cell phone screens. Insufficient melatonin secretion affects sleeping patterns and causes restless sleep. As a result, one does not wake up feeling fresh. It is recommended to put away or switch off all electronic devices at least two hours before bedtime.[24]
- Even during car journeys, encourage your children to not be on the phone, tab or laptop; instead, engage in conversations pertaining to schools, play or friends

to feel more connected with your child. As per my estimation, 'digital intoxication' poses the greatest risk that the world will face in the near future.

I have observed in my practice that children of the present generation are more used to smiling, laughing, crying, dancing, cheering and expressing themselves on their phones, but their faces are blank when they are face to face with someone. Parents are unable to explain the bad effects of this problem as they themselves are on their phones all the time. Children have begun to lose their ability to connect with nature and people around them naturally; virtual space is the only space where they seem able to communicate and express!

How to Handle Exam Stress

Exams hover like ominous clouds over the minds of all school-going children. This stress is also on mothers who are cooped up at home before and during the exams, as if their own exams are going on. But with the right preparation and support from parents, one can smartly manage exam stress and maximize efficiency. This particularly applies to teens from eighth standard onwards.

Below are some of the common patterns that emerge during exams and some simple tips to maximize output, minimize stress and manage the undesirable side effects of exams.

WEIGHT GAIN

Many kids come to me after exams with the common complaint that they gained 3–5 kg just during exams. Weight gain has become an expected outcome of exams.

Listen to me: Parents should encourage their child to engage in free play activity or their favourite sport during study leaves for at least an hour. During exam days too, they should take out around thirty minutes for playtime. As mentioned in the chapter titled 'The Need for Exercise', exercise increases blood flow to the brain. The blood delivers oxygen and glucose, which the brain needs for heightened alertness and mental focus. Hence, exercise will ensure better output during the exam and also arrest the weight gain.

CHOOSING THE WRONG FOODS

Both parents and children view the pre-exam and exam periods as a stressful time and tend to become very irritable and moody. It is common practice for mothers to pamper and motivate their kids with sugar-laden desserts and quick-fix meals like instant noodles or takeaway pizzas.

Listen to me: *Choose your foods smartly: simple carbohydrates like junk food and sugar-laden desserts and drinks can cause drowsiness and decreased alertness. Sometimes, they also make the child hyperactive, irritable and moody. Too much sugary drinks and soda pop may make the child even more anxious. Parents should take special care and pay special attention to their teenager's diet, making it healthier, low on carbohydrates and fat and ensuring that meals are small and frequent in order to provide sustained energy and more brain power to the child. All four major meals should have a combination of carbohydrates, protein and fats, with special emphasis on not omitting but rather lowering the fat content of the meal. Space out breakfast, lunch, snacks and dinner four-hourly, with healthy fillers between the meals. Mid-meal fillers could be fruit, buttermilk, a fistful of nuts, coconut water, soup, carrots, cucumber sticks, etc. Keep the portions controlled and avoid elaborate meals.*

MUNCHING AT NIGHT

Kids tend to snack on packet foods like Kurkure, Pringles, wafers and chocolates and drink aerated drinks, Red Bull, iced tea, tea or coffee while studying at night. This might have an undesirable effect on their weight. It may also lead to acidity, nausea, vomiting and irritability and may make them sick the next day.

Listen to me: Parents should stock their kids' study area with healthier food options like bananas, apples, grapes, berries, nuts and herbal teas. Every cup of tea or coffee should be spaced out with a fruit in between to control acidity and nausea.

STUDYING TILL THE ELEVENTH HOUR

Last-minute study and excessive reading when the mind is tired will not help the child retain information. Instead, a good night's sleep and a rested mind go a long way in enabling better scores. An agitated mind will not remember the information when the time comes to put it down on paper.

Listen to me: The night before the exam, encourage your child to sleep at least eight hours. A minimum of six to eight hours of sleep is required to maximize output during exam time. This should be explained to children beforehand so that they can finish their revision in time and not leave it for the last minute.

FALLING SICK BEFORE OR DURING THE EXAMS

It is not uncommon for kids to fall ill or contract the flu just before or during exam time. Part cause of this is stress due to exams. When the child falls ill, concentration levels are adversely affected and the will to study hard dies. This further adds to the child's stress as he/she becomes worried about completing the syllabus on time.

Listen to me: Start giving your child vitamin C supplements fifteen days before the exams and continue till the end of the exams. Multivitamins with zinc and brahmi may also be given regularly to increase their mental alertness and performance.

Below is a table of my favourite picks for every meal during exam days.

Breakfast	Lunch/ Dinner	Snack	Dessert
Nachni chilla	Hummus wrap	Paneer capsicum toasties	Date and walnut biscuit balls
Oats chilla	Egg cabbage roll	Sprout chaat on bread	Chocolate walnut bites
Protein pancakes	Mexican wrap	Spinach and moong dal dosa	Flavoured yoghurt shot
Creamy egg toast	Palak paneer roll	Mini paneer pizza	Apple vermicelli
Baked beans on toast	Daliya with sprouts	Tomato and paneer bruschetta	Banana delight

Prachi, thirteen years old and a studious and intelligent girl, was always conscious about her weight. She was afraid that she would gain weight during her board exams due to reduced activity. We helped her by correcting her vitamin B12 and vitamin D3 levels and making her aware of her prolactin levels which result in weight gain. She was advised on how to manage her mealtimes along with her hectic studying schedule so that she could lose weight even during her examinations. The outcome was laudable—she lost 5 kg despite exams. Naturally, she became more confident and energetic, with better concentrations levels.

Myth Busters

In over a decade of practice, I have come across many myths that plague parents and often lead to bad decisions regarding which foods to eat, what ingredients to keep in the kitchen, etc. Below are the most prominent of these myths and their explanations.

MYTH 1: KIDS NEED A HIGH-PROTEIN DIET FOR GROWTH

I have seen a growing trend among parents to place more emphasis on high-protein foods in their child's daily diet. But the requirement is actually of high carbohydrates and sufficient protein, though excessive carbohydrates will result in obesity.

MYTH 2: CHILDREN SHOULD BE ONLY ON VERY LOW-FAT MILK

Though many studies say that after the age of two, skim milk should be given to children in order to keep weight in check, I believe a child should consume toned milk (3–3.5 per cent fat), not full milk (which has 6 per cent fat), for the satiation and absorption of fat-soluble vitamins A, D, E and K, and also for physical growth. Research from the University of Virginia actually shows an association between skim milk and weight gain, particularly in children. Research suggests that drinking high-fat milk makes children feel satiated longer so they experience reduced craving for food.[25]

Listen to me: If a child is overweight, then I put him/her on skim/ fat-free milk (0–1 per cent fat) for only three months. If a child is at a risk of becoming overweight or obese in the near future, he/she should be given half-fat and toned milk (1.5–2 per cent fat). Parents should make an effort to cut down the intake of junk foods, instead of cutting down on fat from the milk.

MYTH 3: BROWN/WHOLEWHEAT BREAD IS BETTER FOR MY CHILD THAN WHITE BREAD

To break the myth of what sounds healthy and what actually is healthy, we need to deconstruct what wholewheat bread is. Do you think twice before eating wheat bread and also before serving it to your child every day for breakfast? It's time to step back for a moment and think about whether this so-called healthy wholewheat bread is doing any good to your body.

Wholewheat bread has no added beneficial ingredient that can enhance its nutrition composition. In fact, wholewheat bread has extra gluten in it to get the sponginess. Due to the presence of bran in wheat bread, gluten needs to be stepped up to 14 per cent, whereas white bread has natural gluten content of up to 12 per cent. But extra yeast and sugar is added to the wheat bread to enhance its taste, which in turn increases its calorific value.

Gluten has taken centre stage in the world of nutrition. 'Gluten-free' is a very common word you hear. You may not be suffering from gluten intolerance or celiac disease, which is severe inflammation of the small intestine lining, but your child may have non-celiac gluten sensitivity with symptoms of bloating, gas, irregular bowel movements, acidity, joint pain, rash, fatigue, stomach pain and depression. This will disappear once they shift to a 'gluten-free' diet. Gluten is present in all foods containing wheat, like bread, pasta, noodles, pizza, biscuits, wheat chapattis, baked goods, muffins, cookies and products made from semolina (*rawa/suji*), like *upma*, *dhokla*, etc.

Gluten is definitely present in white bread, but in brown wheat bread, extra gluten powder, yeast and sugar are added which increases its calorific value. So it is in no way a healthier option.[26]

Listen to me: I would prefer white bread over brown bread. And prefer poha, upma, idli, nachni, oats and chapatti over any bread.

MYTH 4: ALL THE COOKING SHOULD BE DONE IN OLIVE OIL

Olive oil has a very low smoking point and is therefore not advisable for Indian cooking. Smoking point is the temperature at which the fat starts breaking down and turns into smoke. Indian cooking is mostly done on medium or high flame. Hence, cooking with olive oil can break down the fat, generate smoke and give food an unpleasant taste. Numerous studies show that olive oil is high in MUFA (monounsaturated fatty acids) and is heart-healthy. What they don't tell you is that all the wonderful benefits are lost by heating olive oil beyond a certain point. Since olive oil contains mainly MUFA and a negligible amount of PUFA (polyunsaturated fatty acids), there are certain essential fatty acids (EFAs), which the body requires for cell growth, hormones and immunity, that can only be obtained from PUFA-rich oil.

An Overview of Nutritional Needs

I. OF CHILDREN (5-11 YEARS OLD)

BASIC GUIDELINES

Kids in this age group are developing teeth, bones and muscles; hence, their nutritional needs are more as compared to adults. They need enough carbohydrates so that protein is spared for growth. The protein requirement of this age group is not more than 15 per cent of their total calorie intake. Their ideal fat requirement is around 25 per cent of their total calorie intake, and carbohydrates make up the remaining 60 per cent to ensure optimal growth and height.

1. Carbohydrate-rich food

Carbohydrates provide instant energy to your child. Although carbohydrates are the ones blamed for obesity, they cannot be completely eliminated from the diet. All cereals like wheat, pearl millet (*bajra*), sorghum (*jowar*), rice, and their products such as wholewheat or white bread, pizza base, pasta, semolina, puffed rice (*kurmura*), biscuits, *roti*, *parathas*, noodles, *poha* (flattened rice), pita bread, etc. are good sources of carbohydrates. Fruits and vegetables are also rich in carbohydrates. All sugars, jaggery (*gur*), caramelized sugar, honey, maple syrup, jams should be consumed in limited quantities, though they are rich in carbohydrates.

2. Protein-rich food

Proteins are known as the power foods for growth and development. Proteins from animal sources such as milk, curd, yoghurt, cheese, paneer, egg, chicken, fish, mutton, etc. come under the first-class protein category. They are known as complete protein.

There are also plant-based proteins like pulses and soya bean. But they are termed as second-class proteins because they don't have all the essential amino acids as opposed to animal sources. Combinations of cereals and pulses make for complete protein options for vegetarians.

3. Fat-rich food

All types of vegetable oils, butter, *ghee* are only fats. Then we have other foods that are also rich in fat, such as nuts and seeds, but have some amount of protein too. All animal-based proteins like paneer, yoghurt, curd, cheese and milk have hidden fats.

II. OF YOUNG ADULTS (11-21 YEARS OLD)

Adolescence is one of the most challenging periods in human development. The relatively uniform growth of childhood is suddenly altered by the spurt in growth.[27] During this period, there are not only major physical changes but also massive transformations at the psychological level.

This is the age when parents' influence takes a back seat and peer influence takes the front seat. Acceptance by peers becomes more important than staying in the good books of parents and teachers and adhering to family values. All these influences also affect eating patterns, thought processes and the choice of food and lifestyle.

As a parent, you need to understand and not refute the changing needs of your child, or else there will be friction and rebellion. If you are not able to come to terms with your child's needs and eating behaviour, then you can consult a nutritionist or a healthcare provider.

Puberty is a process of rapid growth and development during which a child also becomes capable of sexual reproduction. This is a natural process which is initiated by the increased production of reproductive hormones such as estrogens, progesterone and testosterone. In general, girls enter the pubertal phase two years earlier than boys. Girls also gain more fat. Ideally, the percentage of fat is 21–22 per cent for girls, as compared to 15–18 per cent for boys. During puberty, boys gain twice the amount of lean tissue as compared to girls.[28]

1. Girls want size zero

Adolescent girls are preoccupied with their body image, and this leads to dietary manipulations that may have negative consequences. Girls carry the misperception that they are overweight, even if they actually have healthy weight. The prevalence of dieting increases with age among females but decreases with age among males. Weight loss is seen as a sign of extraordinary achievement and self-discipline, whereas weight gain is perceived as unacceptable loss of self-control. Fad diets often lead to problems such as anorexia and bulimia, which are common eating disorders among teens. Repeated episodes of binge eating, followed by compensatory behaviour have started to become a norm among teens.

Listen to me: If parents see any sign of dieting, not eating for long hours or frequent sickness, they must encourage nutrition education and counselling for their children to avoid harmful consequences of the diet.

2. Boys want to take protein shakes

Adolescents often feel uncomfortable with their rapidly changing body, yet at the same time want to be like their more popular peers and role models. As per the recommended dietary allowance, the protein need for adolescents varies from 40 gm to 55 gm per day.[25] Protein powders usually have very high protein content which may burden the kidneys.

Listen to me: Protein shakes and supplements are manufactured keeping adults' needs in mind. Teenagers, on the other hand, are in their crucial growing phase, and the effects of these supplements on their body may not be the same as for adults. Hence, it is better to avoid them.

3. Look out for drug abuse (hookah, cigarettes)

Teenagers are often worried about 'fitting in' with their peers. They adopt habits that demonstrate their quest for autonomy and make them feel more like adults, such as drinking alcohol and smoking cigarettes or hookah.[30] As per the American Lung Association, 'Smoking hookah for an hour is equivalent to smoking a pack of cigarettes, and the amount of tar and nicotine consumption is the same as 1 packet of cigarettes.'[31] Smoking is linked to stunted growth in adolescents and teenagers, and it has irreversible negative effects on height gain and bone growth.

Listen to me: Parents should work on creating a friend-like bond with their child, so that if he/she develops any such unhealthy habits, they become aware of the addiction sooner, and can counsel the child towards getting rid of the addiction.

4. Skipping breakfast

Teenagers tend to wake up just in the nick of time and rush to school, inevitably skipping breakfast. This lowers their basic metabolic rate and could affect their performance at school, while also affecting their immunity in the long run. Because of this, they tend to reach out to junk food.

Listen to me: Make your child aware of the importance of breakfast and make sure you are around when the child is going to school so that he/she doesn't skip breakfast.

5. The prevalence of PCOS among young girls

Polycystic ovary syndrome is the condition of disbalanced hormones in a woman's body. Women having PCOS develop cysts on their ovaries. While these cysts are not dangerous, their effects are. PCOS can cause problems with menstrual cycles and pregnancy, and may also adversely affect one's physical appearance. If left untreated, over time, it can lead to serious health problems, such as diabetes and heart disease.[32]

In a study published in the *BioMed Research International* journal, it was seen that the prevalence of PCOS among Indian adolescent girls (12–19 years old) was higher in the urban population than in the rural.[33] Prevention, early detection and treating at primary level can help prevent health disorders later in life like infertility and obesity. Adolescents who opt for low-fat or crash diets fall prey to the consequences of reduced intake of PUFA, such as PCOS, because PUFA are found in vegetable oils, fish or nuts. According to Dr Nikhil Bhagwat, 'In Indian studies the prevalence of PCOS has increased by 10–20 per cent. . . . faulty lifestyle (lack of physical activity and excessive intake of junk food) leads to this condition. Weight loss is the key in this scenario. One can correct this with nutrition, a multi-discipline regime, exercise and by consulting an endocrinologist, a gynaecologist or a nutrition expert' (Private communication, 13 October 2015).

Listen to me: I suggest that a low-carbohydrate and well-balanced protein and fat diet works best for girls suffering from PCOS. Supplementation with chromium helps them to metabolize sugar better. Incorporating at least 2–3 tsp of vegetable oil such as sunflower, peanut, rice bran, etc. for seasoning will help them to get the required amount of PUFA in their diet.

6. Acne among teens

Acne is triggered by the increase of certain hormones during adolescence. This stimulates the fat glands in the skin to step up the production of sebum (oily secretion), which tends to clog the skin. Teenagers should be made aware of the reasons for the occurrence of acne. Diet could be one of the factors, apart from hormonal changes, stress and the stage of menstrual cycle.[34] As also mentioned in the following chapter, 'Mighty Minerals and Vital Vitamins', vitamin D levels should be kept under check to prevent acne among teens. I have observed that another reason for acne is high consumption of refined grains and breads, as they spike up insulin levels and trigger sebaceous glands to produce oil and clog the pores. According to Dr Malvika Kohli, MD, DVD, DNB, 'Acne vulgaris commonly affects 70–80 per cent of adolescents and young adults. It is a skin condition involving the oil glands at the base of the hair follicles. It starts during puberty when the oil glands become active and are stimulated by male hormones (androgens) produced by adrenal glands in both males and females. Androgens cause oil glands to enlarge and produce more sebum.

As far as diet and acne is concerned, no single food causes acne or treats its symptoms, but it could improve or worsen its severity. Many dietary factors influence hormones, growth factors and sebum production. Insulin and high glycaemic index diets are two factors most scientifically and clinically associated with acne' (Private communication, 13 October 2015).

Listen to me: Parents should check the D3 levels, insulin production and other hormones as well as the junk food intake of their child. Visiting a skin specialist, endocrinologist and nutritionist can also help in covering all bases in dealing with acne.

BASIC GUIDELINES

The energy requirement for teenagers varies according to age, sex, pubertal growth and physical activity. It is very difficult to give a specific number to it. The energy intake should not be more than the energy expenditure or else it will result in weight gain. But a low-carbohydrate diet will result in stunted growth, and delayed puberty.

Deficiency of protein is not generally seen in teenagers who are non-vegetarians, but could be seen in high-carbohydrate vegetarian diets. Protein requirement of growing children is not more than 15 per cent of their total calorie intake. Vegetarian teenagers who consume approximately 800 ml of milk or milk products per day do not need to overemphasize on protein intake as the protein present in milk takes care of 70 per cent of the overall protein requirement. The rest comes from one or two cups of dal or from other sources.

Fats are an inevitable problem for all ages, but especially during this phase. Fat should ideally be around 25 per cent of total body mass. Too little fat can cause stunted growth, dry skin, thinning of hair, weakened immune system and delayed menstruation.

Listen to me: *Eggs can be cooked in olive oil or can be used as salad dressing. The rest of the cooking should be done in normal cooking oil for balance of PUFA, MUFA and saturated fatty acids (SFAs). The SFA requirement for teenagers can be fulfilled by milk and milk products, chicken and fish.*

Neena Shah (name changed), sixteen, visited my clinic, her diet devoid of any fat. Though her menstrual cycles started when she was twelve, after this low-fat diet, her cycles stopped altogether. Her body fat percentage was less than 12 per cent. With the reintroduction of 3–4 tsp of fat in her diet, her cycles returned to normal.

In April 2012, Sharan, a sixteen-year-old boy, came to me for increasing his height, losing weight and getting help on how to ensure well-balanced meals. His height was 175 cm. Teenage boys gain height till the age of 21 through the right balance of nutrients in their diet. He was a non-vegetarian and did not have any medical issues. During consultation, I realized that his diet had good amount of dairy and meat, but the distribution of meals and exercise was the problem. We recommended a few blood tests which revealed vitamin deficiencies.

Quick intervention was taken with multivitamins. In a short span of time, he gained 4.5 cm of height and lost 4 kg.

Mighty Minerals and Vital Vitamins

Nowadays, it is important to supplement your diet with vitamins and minerals to ensure good and vibrant health, instead of waiting for a deficiency to crop up and facing its negative consequences.

Considering the hectic schedules of working parents, wholesome homemade food is not always possible. Even after having wholesome, freshly cooked meals, kids might not receive the required vitamins due to high levels of pollution, preservation techniques in packaged foods, pasteurization of food products and quick cooking methods.

MIGHTY MINERALS

1. IRON

Iron deficiency is the most common nutrient disorder in schoolgoing children. Parents should take special care in this regard as iron deficiency leads to decreased attention span, poor concentration and low immunity. Iron deficiency is quite common due to low bio-availability of iron in vegetarian food. Iron deficiency poses higher risk for girls after their menstrual cycles begin. The daily requirement of iron doubles for adolescent females and increases by 1½ times for adolescent males during this period.

Listen to me: Encourage kids to choose foods rich in iron like pulses, pistachios and dates. Though leafy vegetables like spinach, amaranth and cauliflower are high in iron content, due to the oxalate content in these, the absorption of iron is poor. Meat, egg and fish are rich sources of iron. But if any deficiencies are observed in the child, then it might become necessary to give him/her iron supplements along with a vitamin C supplement for better absorption.

2. CALCIUM

The Indian recommended dietary allowance (RDA) says that around 800 mg of calcium is required for children aged 10–17 years old. While the calcium requirement for preschool- and schoolgoing children is 600 mg, after the age of 11, the requirement rises up to 1,200–1,300 mg.[35] Calcium is important for bone and skeletal development. In children of ages between 12 and 14 years, there is formation of about 20 per cent of the total bone mineral content found in adulthood.

Listen to me: If 600 ml of dairy protein is consumed by schoolgoing children, and 800 ml by adolescents, the requirement of calcium is met. If the child is severely lactose-intolerant or is a vegan, then a calcium supplement should be considered, but only after confirming with a paediatrician.

3. ZINC

Zinc is known to be essential for growth and sexual maturation. Although there has been limited research on this, there is some evidence that adolescents with low serum zinc levels may have increased problems of acne.[36] Zinc deficiency demonstrates symptoms like depressed immunity, growth failure, anorexia, diarrhoea and altered skeletal functions.[37] One study conducted amongst adolescents in Delhi concluded that, overall, 49.4 per cent children were found to have zinc deficiency.[38] Children who are vegetarian or who consume a lot of processed foods tend to be at a higher risk of zinc deficiency. Hence, zinc supplementation for these children can be beneficial.

Listen to me: *Supplement your teenager's diet with multivitamins which have zinc.*

VITAL VITAMINS

1. THE BENEFICIAL Bs

The need for vitamins is more during adolescence because of increased energy demands during this period. Increased quantities of vitamins B1, B2 and B3 are required for energy release from carbohydrates. With tissue synthesis, there is an increase in demand for vitamins B6 and B12 and folic acid. Apart from the beneficial Bs, the vitamins A, C and E are required for new cell growth.[39]

Listen to me: *I would suggest that you give your schoolgoing child and adolescent a multivitamin every day.*

2. SUNSHINE VITAMIN

Vitamin D is required for better calcium and phosphorus absorption which is in turn required for bone development and attaining optimum height. Deficiency of vitamin D can cause insulin resistance, acne, patchy skin, hormonal imbalance and low immunity, early onset of diabetes and problems with blood pressure. In my practice, I have seen that a lot of kids are deficient in vitamin D3 as there is less exposure to sun, limited outdoor activity and high pollution in metro cities. Low amounts of vitamin D in your system can also increase oil production in your skin cells. Acne forms when the sebaceous glands are clogged and these blocked oil-producing cells lead to unsightly blemishes that can afflict you at any time in your life. Therefore, besides giving zinc supplements, vitamin D3 should also be added to the diet.[40]

The daily recommended dose of vitamin D as per the Institute of Medicine, USA, is 600 international units per day;[41] as per the Indian RDA, it is 200 units per day.

95 percent of the children who come to me are vitamin-deficient, the most common deficiency being that of vitamin D.

Listen to me: *Parents are advised to make sure that D3 levels of children are checked every year and supplemented after consulting a doctor or nutritionist. However, taking an injection of D3 with a high dose is not recommended.*

Dr Neeru Vithalani (MBBS, MD, Paediatrics), renowned paediatrician of Mumbai, says, 'Vitamin D is the most commonly seen deficiency, attributed to low dietary calcium along with skin pigmentation, physical agents blocking UVR exposure, clothing, latitude, season, air pollution, cloud cover, altitude, changing lifestyle and strict vegan diet. I strongly recommend vitamin D supplementation and other supplements depending on individual diet and lifestyle to schoolgoing children in Mumbai' (Private communication, 25 March 2015).

Nowadays, vitamin D (60 K) is also available in the form of chewy tablets. I have used vitamin D3 supplements to help children with skin problems. As soon as their deficiency was corrected, their skin texture and colour improved.

Twelve-year-old Beena, a schoolgoing girl, complained of weight gain and felt tired after a long day at school. We asked her to take a few tests for vitamins such as B12 and D3, and corrected the deficiencies we found with the right supplementation. A thoughtfully designed diet helped her lose 6.5 kg in three months along with gain in her height. Eating healthy and exercising regularly made her feel more energetic and changed her lifestyle at a young age, which would also reduce the chances of any health issues later in life.

Part 2

Recipes

Conversion Chart

WEIGHT CONVERSIONS

1 kg = 2.2 pounds

1 ounce (oz) = 28.3 gm

VOLUME CONVERSIONS

1 cup = 200 ml

¾ cup = 150 ml

½ cup = 100 ml

1 soup bowl = 1½ cups

⅓ cup = 80 ml

1 tsp + 1 tsp + 1 tsp = 1 tbsp

1 tsp = 5 ml

1 tbsp = 15 ml

30 ml = 1 oz

8 pinches = 1 tsp

1 tbsp + 1 tbsp = 1 fluid ounce (fl. oz)

WEIGHT–VOLUME EQUIVALENTS
Vegetables

Vegetable	Large (gm)	Medium (gm)	Small (gm)
1 onion	100	60	40
1 tomato	130	75	60
1 potato	150	80	60
1 capsicum	100	70	50

 1 bundle of spinach = 110 gm (after cleaning)

 1 packet of mushrooms = 200 gm

 5 big mushrooms = 100 gm

 8 big baby corns = 100 gm

 1 cup sweet corn = 100 gm

Flour/Cereals

 50 gm uncooked noodles = 1 cup (100 gm) cooked noodles

 1 cup wheat flour (*atta*) = 100 gm

1 cup sorghum (*jowar*) flour = 90 gm

1 cup all-purpose flour (*maida*) = 80 gm

 1 cup broken wheat (*dalia*) = 120 gm

 1 cup semolina (*rawa/suji*) = 130 gm

 1 cup uncooked rice (200 gm) = 3 cups cooked rice (550 gm)

1 cup puffed rice (*kurmura*) = 20 gm

 50 gm uncooked pasta = 100 gm cooked pasta

Dairy

 = 80 gm paneer

 = 125 gm paneer

Cooking Terminology

Dice	Cut into small cubes
Drizzle	Moisten with fine drops of a liquid
Desiccated	Dried and powdered
Grease	Coat with little oil/butter
Julienned	Cut into long, thin strips ⅛ inch in thickness
Marinate	Coat with or soak foods in a liquid and allow to stand before cooking to tenderize and enhance their flavour
Muslin cloth	A finely woven white cotton cloth
Puree	Process food in a blender to form a thick, smooth sauce
Quartered	Divided into four equal parts
Roast	Cook dry by heating or in an oven
Sauté	Fry briefly in a small amount of hot fat, tossing frequently

Shelf life	The length of time a product can safely be stored before it becomes unsuitable for consumption
Simmer	Cook slowly, bubbling gently in a liquid just below boiling point
Slit	Cut lengthwise into long pieces or strips
Spatula	A kitchen tool with a handle at one end and a wide flat part at the other used for lifting, spreading, or stirring foods
Splutter	The cracking sound when something (usually seeds) is fried in oil to release its flavour
Stir-fry	Fry swiftly in a small amount of fat/oil over high flame, stirring constantly to ensure uniform cooking
Strain	Separate solids from liquids by passing through a strainer/sieve

Breakfast

Introduction

A wholesome breakfast can keep you alert, happy and contented throughout the day. Breakfast should have the right balance of carbohydrates, proteins, fats and fibre. This breakfast menu has been designed with the right combination of all these nutrients. Along with this, there are 'brain-boosting' ingredients in each recipe, like yoghurt, eggs, spinach and pulses, which boost brainpower and help your child perform well in his studies. It is important to combine carbohydrates and proteins in breakfast so that there is slow energy release and your child does not get drowsy in class. I am sure you won't receive any complaints of your child not paying attention in class after you fill your little one's stomach with these wholesome, healthy, unjunked breakfast recipes. These recipes are not only carefully balanced but also supreme in taste. Even proper junk food like *vada pav* has been unjunked.

My personal favourites are Creamy Egg Toast, Oats Pancake, Paneer Toastie, Zucchini Mushroom Sandwich . . . and how can I forget the Baked Vada Pav!

Baked Vada Pav

The baked version of everyone's favourite Maharashtrian street food.

MAKES: 8
SERVING SIZE: 2

PREPARATION TIME: 10 mins
COOKING TIME: 20 mins

INGREDIENTS
8 slices white/wholewheat bread
125 gm paneer (see recipe on p. 237)
4 medium potatoes, boiled and mashed lightly
3–4 garlic cloves, chopped finely
3–4 green chillies, chopped finely
2 tbsp fresh coriander leaves, chopped finely
1-inch piece of ginger, julienned
10–15 curry leaves
½ tsp mustard seeds
½ tsp turmeric powder
1 tbsp oil
Juice of 1 lemon
Salt as per taste

METHOD
1. Preheat the oven at 160° C for 7–10 minutes.
2. Use a small cookie cutter of approximately 3-inch diameter to cut a round of each bread slice. Keep aside.
3. Heat oil in a pan and add mustard seeds. Once the

seeds begin to splutter, tip in the garlic, green chillies, ginger, turmeric powder and curry leaves. Sauté for a few seconds.

4. Add the potatoes and salt. Mix well.
5. Crumble the paneer and combine with the potato mix, along with coriander leaves, and lemon juice. Keep aside.
6. Lightly toast the bread rounds in the preheated oven for 2–3 minutes.
7. Spread ⅓ cup of the potato mix on each toasted round and bake in the oven for 5 minutes.
8. To serve, make a smiley with ketchup and serve with green chutney.

Complete your plate—with a fruit or a glass of freshly squeezed fruit juice.

VALUE PER SERVING (2 VADA PAVS)

Calories	299 kcal
Protein	9 gm
Fat	12 gm
Carbohydrates	33 gm
Fibre	1 gm
Calcium	345 mg
Iron	1 mg

Corn and Spinach Toast

A quick and easy dish for that early morning rush!

MAKES: 5
SERVING SIZE: 1

PREPARATION TIME: 5 mins
COOKING TIME: 15 mins

INGREDIENTS
5 slices white/wholewheat bread
1 cup corn (from cob) or sweet corn kernels
1 cup spinach, chopped finely
30 gm cheese, grated
1½ cup toned milk
2 tbsp cornflour
¼ tsp black pepper powder
1 tbsp butter
Salt as per taste
1 tsp dried oregano (optional; for garnishing)
1 tsp red chilli flakes (optional; for garnishing)

METHOD
1. Preheat the oven at 160° C for 7–10 minutes.
2. Meanwhile, pressure-cook the sweet corn for 4 whistles. Drain.
3. Mix ¼ tsp salt with the chopped spinach and keep aside for 10 minutes.
4. Churn half of the sweet corn in a mixer for one quick whisk and keep aside.

5. Heat butter in a pan. Squeeze out all the excess water from the spinach and add to the pan. Sauté for 2 minutes.
6. Add 1 cup milk to the above. Let it boil. Meanwhile, add the cornflour to ½ cup (100 ml) cold milk to make a paste; then add it to the above. Keep stirring constantly to prevent lumps from forming.
7. When the mixture reaches a semi-thick consistency, add the black pepper powder, churn it and add the boiled corn and salt as per taste. Mix well.
8. After a few seconds, turn off the flame and mix in the cheese.
9. Lightly toast the bread slices in a toaster or preheated oven for 2–3 minutes.
10. Spread ⅓ cup of the mixture on each toasted bread.
11. Garnish with oregano and red chilli flakes. Bake in preheated oven for 5–7 minutes. Serve hot.

Complete your plate—with a glass of milkshake.

VALUE PER SERVING (1 TOAST)

Calories	181 kcal
Protein	7 gm
Fat	7 gm
Carbohydrates	22 gm
Fibre	1 gm
Calcium	150 mg
Iron	1 mg

Creamy Egg Toast

Protein-rich egg whites cooked with vegetables and white sauce served on toast.

MAKES: 6
SERVING SIZE: 2

PREPARATION TIME: 5 mins
COOKING TIME: 15 mins

INGREDIENTS
6 slices white/wholewheat bread
4 eggs
1 medium onion, chopped finely
3 baby corns, chopped finely
½ large red bell pepper, chopped finely
½ large capsicum, chopped finely
¾ cup toned milk
2 tsp cornflour
½ tsp powdered sugar
½ tsp red chilli flakes
1 tbsp dried mixed herbs (Italian seasoning)
3 tbsp cheese, grated (optional)
¼ tsp black pepper powder
2 tbsp oil
Salt as per taste

METHOD
1. Preheat the oven at 160° C for 7–10 minutes.
2. Meanwhile, hard-boil the eggs. Scoop out the yolk; it is

not required in this recipe. Chop the boiled egg whites into small cubes.

3. Bring 2 cups water to a boil and add the baby corn. Cook for 3 minutes until the corn is just tender. Strain and keep aside.
4. Take ¼ cup milk and add cornflour to it to make a paste.
5. In a separate vessel, heat the remaining milk for the white sauce.
6. After 2 minutes, add the cornflour paste to the milk. Keep stirring constantly to prevent lumps from forming.
7. When it reaches a semi-thick consistency, add sugar. Remove from heat and keep the white sauce aside.
8. Heat the oil in a pan. Sauté the onions until they turn translucent.
9. Add capsicum and bell pepper; sauté for 3 minutes.
10. Add baby corn, black pepper powder and salt as per taste; sauté for another 2 minutes.
11. Add the chopped egg white cubes; sauté for 1 minute.
12. Stir in the white sauce and cook for another minute. Turn off the flame.
13. Sprinkle chilli flakes, dried herbs and cheese.
14. Lightly toast the bread slices in a toaster or preheated oven for 2–3 minutes.
15. Spread ⅓ cup of the egg filling on each toast. Bake it in the preheated oven for 5–7 minutes. Serve hot.

Complete your plate—with a bowl of mixed fruits.

VALUE PER SERVING (2 TOASTS)

Calories	224 kcal
Protein	10 gm
Fat	7 gm
Carbohydrates	28 gm
Fibre	2 gm
Calcium	151 mg
Iron	0.5 mg

Herbed Beans on Toast

The classic baked beans on toast tossed in herbed salsa sauce.

MAKES: 12
SERVING SIZE: 2

PREPARATION TIME: 10 mins
COOKING TIME: 20 mins

INGREDIENTS
12–14 slices white/wholewheat bread
2 cups canned baked beans
1 large onion, chopped finely
1 medium capsicum, chopped finely
¾ cup cabbage, chopped finely
¾ cup greens of spring onion, chopped finely
½ cup pasta–pizza/salsa sauce (see recipe on p. 239)
2 tbsp tomato ketchup
1½ tbsp dried mixed herbs (Italian seasoning)
1 tsp red chilli flakes
¼ tsp black pepper powder
1 tbsp oil
Salt as per taste
¾ cup cabbage, shredded (for garnishing)
40 gm cheese, grated (for garnishing)

METHOD
1. Preheat the oven at 160° C for 7–10 minutes.
2. Meanwhile, heat oil in a pan. Sauté the onions until translucent.

3. Add the capsicum and sauté for 2 minutes.
4. Add the cabbage and spring onion greens. Sprinkle ½ tsp salt. Sauté for 1 minute.
5. Lightly mash the baked beans and add to the above mix. Cook for 1 minute.
6. Add the salsa/pasta–pizza sauce, black pepper powder and salt as per taste. Cook for another 2 minutes.
7. Add the dried mixed herbs and chilli flakes. Remove from heat and keep aside.
8. Lightly toast the bread slices in a toaster or a preheated oven for 2–3 minutes.
9. Spread ⅓ cup of the beans mix on each toast.
10. Bake it in the preheated oven for 5–7 minutes.
11. Garnish with grated cheese and shredded cabbage before serving. Serve hot.

It's a complete plate!

VALUE PER SERVING (2 TOASTS)

Calories	281 kcal
Protein	13 gm
Fat	8 gm
Carbohydrates	39 gm
Fibre	2 gm
Calcium	194 mg
Iron	1 mg

Oats Pancake

The goodness of high-fibre oats combined with lots of veggies and curd to make a wholesome breakfast.

MAKES: 6
SERVING SIZE: 2

PREPARATION TIME: 10 mins
COOKING TIME: 15 mins

INGREDIENTS
1½ cups instant oats
1½ cups fresh curd
⅓ cup onion, chopped finely
⅓ cup carrots, grated finely
⅓ cup cabbage, chopped finely
¼ cup tomato, chopped finely
¼ cup capsicum, chopped finely
¼ cup French beans, sliced thinly
3 green chillies, chopped finely
3 tbsp fresh coriander leaves, chopped finely
4½ tsp oil
Salt as per taste

METHOD
1. Combine the oats and curd. Rest the batter for 10 minutes.
2. Add to the batter all the vegetables, green chillies, coriander leaves, ⅓ cup water and salt as per taste. Mix thoroughly. Rest for another 10 minutes.

3. Heat a non-stick pan, lower the flame and pour ½ cup batter in the pan to make a pancake of about 4 inches in diameter.
4. Drizzle ½ tsp oil along the sides of the pancake and let it cook over a low flame till the bottom turns golden brown. Flip over and cook the other side with another ¼ tsp oil in the same way.
5. Repeat with the remaining batter to make five more pancakes.
6. Serve hot with coriander chutney and/or ketchup.

Complete your plate—with a fruit or a glass of freshly squeezed fruit juice.

VALUE PER SERVING (2 PANCAKES)

Calories	262 kcal
Protein	9 gm
Fat	12 gm
Carbohydrates	28 gm
Fibre	4 gm
Calcium	174 mg
Iron	2 mg

Paneer Toastie

A perfectly balanced breakfast with proteins, carbohydrates, fibre and calcium.

MAKES: 6
SERVING SIZE: 1

PREPARATION TIME: 5 mins
COOKING TIME: 15 mins

INGREDIENTS
12 slices white/wholewheat bread
125 gm paneer (see recipe on p. 237), grated
½ cup green peas, shelled
½ cup fresh corn (from cob) or sweet corn kernels
½ cup carrots, grated finely
¾ cup spinach, chopped finely
1 medium onion, chopped finely
1 small zucchini
1 tbsp ginger–green chilli paste (see recipe on p. 238)
1 tbsp butter
½ tsp black pepper powder
Salt as per taste

METHOD
1. Combine the peas and corn and pressure-cook for 3 whistles with a little salt. Drain and mash lightly. Keep aside.
2. Heat butter in a pan. Sauté the ginger–green chilli paste for 1 minute.

3. Add the onions; sauté till translucent.
4. Add carrots; sauté for 2 minutes.
5. Add spinach; sauté for another 3–4 minutes.
6. Add the mashed peas and corn and season with black pepper powder and salt as per taste.
7. Add the grated paneer to the above mixture. Remove from heat and keep aside.
8. Peel the zucchini and cut into slices about ½ cm thick.
9. Heat a non-stick pan and dry-roast the zucchini slices on both sides until they turn brownish.
10. To make the sandwich, take one slice of bread and layer with a few roasted zucchini slices.
11. Put ⅓ cup of the paneer mix and cover with another slice of bread. You can grill or toast the sandwich.
12. Cut each toastie into two triangles and serve with ketchup.

It's a complete plate!

VALUE PER SERVING (1 TOASTIE)

Calories	236 kcal
Protein	9 gm
Fat	9 gm
Carbohydrates	27 gm
Fibre	1 gm
Calcium	270 mg
Iron	1 mg

Ragi Veggie Uttapam

The goodness of ragi combined with vegetables and sprouts to make a healthy and nutritious uttapam.

MAKES: **10**
SERVING SIZE: **2**

PRE-PREPARATION TIME: **6–8 hrs**
PREPARATION TIME: **10 mins**
COOKING TIME: **15 mins**

INGREDIENTS
1 cup red millet flour
½ cup rice flour
½ cup semolina
1 cup fresh curd
¾ cup green gram sprouts or ¼ cup uncooked green gram
(Pre-prep: Soak for 6–8 hours, drain and keep covered)
1 medium tomato, chopped finely
½ cup spinach, chopped finely
½ cup cabbage, chopped finely
½ cup carrots, peeled and grated finely
½ cup bottle gourd, grated finely
1½ tsp turmeric powder
1 tbsp ginger–green chilli paste
5 tsp oil
Salt as per taste

METHOD

1. In a bowl, combine all the ingredients except oil. Mix thoroughly to form a smooth batter. Add water only if required.

2. Heat a non-stick pan, lower the flame and pour ⅓ cup batter in the pan to make an *uttapam* of about 4 inches in diameter.

3. Drizzle ¼ tsp oil along the sides of the *uttapam* and let it cook over a low flame till the bottom turns golden brown. Flip over and cook the other side with another ¼ tsp oil in the same way.

4. Repeat with the remaining batter to make four more *uttapam*s.

5. Serve with green chutney and/or ketchup.

Complete your plate—with a glass of buttermilk.

VALUE PER SERVING (2 UTTAPAMS)

Calories	302 kcal
Protein	7 gm
Fat	9 gm
Carbohydrates	38 gm
Fibre	1 gm
Calcium	176 mg
Iron	2 mg

Savoury Protein Pancakes

A high-protein pancake to kick-start your day the right way!

MAKES: 8
SERVING SIZE: 2

PRE-PREPARATION TIME: 2 hrs
PREPARATION TIME: 10 mins
COOKING TIME: 35 mins

INGREDIENTS
¾ cup uncooked yellow or green gram **(Pre-prep: Soak for 2 hours)**
½ cup semolina
½ cup bean sprouts
¼ cup onion, chopped finely
¼ cup tomato, chopped finely
¼ cup capsicum, chopped finely
¼ cup cabbage, chopped finely
¼ cup carrots, grated finely
½ cup spinach, chopped finely
4 green chillies, chopped coarsely
½-inch piece of ginger, chopped coarsely
4 tbsp fresh curd
½ tsp turmeric powder
3 tbsp oil
1 tsp salt (or as per taste)

METHOD

1. Rinse and drain the soaked dal. Grind in a mixer with green chillies, ginger and ¼ cup water. Pour the batter into a large bowl.
2. Add semolina and mix thoroughly.
3. Add ¼ tsp salt to the chopped spinach and keep it aside for 10 minutes. Then squeeze out all excess water from the spinach.
4. To the semolina mix, add all the chopped vegetables, spinach, bean sprouts, curd, turmeric powder and salt as per taste. Add ¼ cup water; if required, add more water until the batter reaches a semi-thick consistency.
5. Rest the batter for 15–20 minutes.
6. Heat a non-stick pan, lower the flame and pour ⅓ cup batter in the pan to make a pancake of about 4 inches in diameter.
7. Drizzle ½ tsp oil along the sides of the pancake and let it cook over a low flame till the bottom turns golden brown. Flip over and cook the other side with another ½ tsp oil in the same way.
8. Flip the pancake, again drizzle ½ tsp oil and cook until golden brown.
9. Repeat with the remaining batter to make seven more pancakes.
10. Serve hot with green chutney and/or ketchup.

Complete your plate—with a fruit or a glass of freshly squeezed fruit juice.

VALUE PER SERVING (2 PANCAKES)

Calories	236 kcal
Protein	9 gm
Fat	9 gm
Carbohydrates	30 gm
Fibre	1 gm
Calcium	60 mg
Iron	2 mg

Vegetable Junglee Sandwich

A healthy sandwich of veggies and mayo. . . . Pack it and have it on the go!

MAKES: **5**
SERVING SIZE: **1**

PRE-PREPARATION TIME: **90 mins**
PREPARATION TIME: **10 mins**
COOKING TIME: **10 mins**

INGREDIENTS
10 slices white/wholewheat bread
2 cups fresh curd **(Pre-prep: Hang in a muslin cloth for 90 minutes)**
½ cup carrots, chopped finely
½ cup French beans, chopped finely
¼ cup red cabbage, chopped finely
¼ cup fresh parsley, chopped finely
¼ cup green peas, shelled
½ cup garlic mayonnaise*
10 large, curled lettuce leaves
2 tsp powdered sugar
½ tsp mustard seeds
4–5 curry leaves
1 tsp oil
½ tsp black pepper powder
Salt as per taste

---

* An easy replacement of readymade garlic mayo can be prepared by adding ½ tbsp grated garlic to ½ cup mayo.

METHOD

1. Pressure-cook the peas for 2 whistles. Drain and keep aside.
2. Boil the carrots and French beans in water for 5–7 minutes, drain, then squeeze the water completely and keep aside.
3. Remove the hung curd from the cloth and transfer to a large bowl.
4. To the curd, add garlic mayonnaise, boiled carrots, French beans and boiled peas.
5. Then add red cabbage, parsley, black pepper powder, sugar and salt as per taste. Mix well and keep aside.
6. Heat the oil and add the mustard seeds. Once the seeds begin to splutter, turn off the flame and immediately add the curry leaves to make a sort of *tadka*.
7. Add this *tadka* to the mayonnaise mix. Divide the mix into five equal portions.
8. Take one slice of bread and put one lettuce leaf on it. Top with one portion of the mayonnaise mix and again put one lettuce leaf on it. Cover with another slice. Cut each sandwich into two halves and serve.
9. Similarly prepare the remaining four sandwiches.

Complete your plate—with a fruit or a glass of freshly squeezed fruit juice.

VALUE PER SERVING (1 SANDWICH)

Calories	244 kcal
Protein	8 gm
Fat	11 gm
Carbohydrates	39 gm
Calcium	113 mg
Fibre	2 gm
Iron	1 mg

Zucchini and Mushroom Sandwich

An exotic sandwich with a perfect balance of calcium, protein and energy.

MAKES: 4
SERVING SIZE: 1

PREPARATION TIME: **10 mins**
COOKING TIME: **10 mins**

INGREDIENTS
8 slices white/wholewheat bread
50 gm paneer (see recipe on p. 237), grated
¾ cup zucchini, unpeeled, halved length-wise and sliced thinly
1 cup mushrooms, sliced thinly
1½ cups spinach, chopped finely
1 cup lettuce leaves, coarsely torn
2–3 garlic cloves, chopped finely
1 tbsp fresh basil leaves, chopped finely (optional)
8 tsp hot and sweet tomato ketchup
½ tsp black pepper powder
1 tbsp oil
Salt as per taste

METHOD
1. Mix ½ tsp salt with the chopped spinach; keep aside for 10 minutes.
2. Heat oil in a pan. Add garlic and sauté until brown.

3. Add zucchini and sauté for 2 minutes.
4. Add mushrooms, black pepper powder and salt as per taste; sauté for another 2 minutes.
5. Squeeze out the excess water from the spinach and add the spinach to the above mix along with basil leaves; sauté for 2 minutes.
6. Add the grated paneer; sauté for another minute.
7. Remove the mixture from the flame and set aside to cool. Divide the filling into four equal portions.
8. Spread 1 tsp hot and sweet tomato ketchup on each slice of bread.
9. Spread one portion of the filling on one bread slice.
10. Put the torn lettuce leaves over the filling and cover with the other slice.
11. Cut the sandwich into two or four triangular pieces and serve. Repeat for the remaining three sandwiches.

Complete your plate — with a fruit or a glass of freshly squeezed fruit juice.

VALUE PER SERVING (1 SANDWICH)

Calories	211 kcal
Protein	7 gm
Fat	8 gm
Carbohydrates	26 gm
Fibre	0.5 gm
Calcium	197 mg
Iron	1 mg

Tiffin

Introduction

For schoolgoing children, tiffin is loved and hated in equal measure. From kids polishing it off in the first period to growing up and considering carrying it as uncool—mums bear the burden of the tricky tiffin. Tiffin is something that your child eats without your supervision. It is also a very important meal which cannot be missed because of long school hours. The following tiffin recipes are easy to prepare, portion-controlled, tasty and with goodness of vital nutrients, which will satisfy your child's hunger. Kids these days do not sit for long to complete a meal, hence wraps and rolls are handy and relished by them. Even teenagers will eat a wrap or a roll but not get their hands dirty eating veggies with a paratha. Eggs, paneer, kidney beans and rainbow-coloured stir-fried vegetables make the meal more interesting and satiating for kids. The flavours of *vada*, *samosa* and fries have been thoughtfully infused in these healthy recipes so that your kids won't reach out for unhealthy fried *samosa*s and *vada*s. My personal favourites in this section are Chinese *idli* sauté, peas and cheese paratha and sweet and sour dragon roll.

Aloo Matar Paneer Roll

A classic wrap for kids combining potato, peas and paneer.

MAKES: **12**
SERVING SIZE: **2**

PREPARATION TIME: **5 mins**
COOKING TIME: **25 mins**

INGREDIENTS
12 basic wraps (see recipe on p. 235)
200 gm paneer (see recipe on p. 237)
2 large potatoes, boiled
1 cup green peas, shelled
2 tbsp fresh coriander leaves, finely chopped
1 tsp cumin seeds
½ tsp turmeric powder
1 ½ tsp red chilli powder
2 tsp coriander powder
¼ tsp *garam masala*
1 tsp *chaat masala*
1 tsp dry mango powder
1 tsp cumin powder
Salt as per taste
1 tbsp oil

METHOD
1. Pressure-cook the peas with 2 cups water for 1 whistle. Drain and keep aside.
2. Dice the paneer and potatoes into tiny cubes.

3. Heat oil in a pan. Add the cumin seeds. When the seeds begin to splutter, add the boiled peas and sauté for a minute.
4. Add turmeric powder, red chilli powder, coriander powder and salt. Sauté for another minute.
5. Add *garam masala*, *chaat masala*, dry mango powder and cumin powder. Sauté for a minute.
6. Add the paneer and potato cubes along with coriander leaves, sauté for a minute, then remove from heat.
7. To make the roll, warm each basic wrap, spread ⅓ cup of the filling in its centre and roll up tightly.
8. Wrap the roll in foil to keep it hot.

It's a complete plate!

VALUE PER SERVING (2 ROLLS)

Calories	370 kcal
Protein	13 gm
Fat	15 gm
Carbohydrates	40 gm
Fibre	2 gm
Calcium	409 mg
Iron	3 mg

Cheesy-Peasy Corn Roll

Our version of a frankie with a tasty filling of cheese, corn and paneer.

MAKES: **12**
SERVING SIZE: **2**

PREPARATION TIME: **25 mins**
COOKING TIME: **10 mins**

INGREDIENTS
12 basic wraps (see recipe on p. 235)
200 gm paneer (see recipe on p. 237)
1 cup corn (from cob) or sweet corn kernels
2 medium onions, chopped finely
1 large capsicum, chopped finely
1 large red bell pepper, chopped finely
1 large potato, boiled, peeled and diced
2 green chillies, chopped finely
4 tbsp fresh coriander leaves, chopped finely
2 tsp *chaat masala*
1 tsp dry mango powder
¼ cup cheese, grated
1½ tbsp oil
Salt as per taste

METHOD
1. Pressure-cook the sweet corn with 2 cups water for 4 whistles. Drain and keep aside.
2. Heat oil in a pan. Add green chillies and onions; sauté

until the onions turn translucent.

3. Add capsicum and red bell peppers; sauté for about 2 minutes.
4. Add the potato, corn, *chaat masala*, dry mango powder and salt; sauté for another minute.
5. Dice the paneer into tiny cubes and add it along with coriander leaves; sauté for another minute.
6. Remove from heat. Add the grated cheese and mix well.
7. To make the roll, warm each basic wrap. Spread ⅓ cup of the corn and paneer mix in the centre of each basic wrap and roll up tightly.
8. Wrap the roll in a foil to keep it hot.

It's a complete plate!

VALUE PER SERVING (2 ROLLS)

Calories	414 kcal
Protein	14 gm
Fat	19 gm
Carbohydrates	41 gm
Fibre	2 gm
Calcium	458 mg
Iron	2 mg

Chana Kebab Roll

Protein-rich chickpea kebabs and crunchy veggies packed in a roll.

MAKES: 6
SERVING SIZE: 2

PRE-PREPARATION TIME: 6–8 hrs
PREPARATION TIME: 20 mins
COOKING TIME: 60 mins

INGREDIENTS
6 basic wraps (see recipe on p. 235)
½ cup uncooked chickpeas **(Pre-prep: Soak for 6–8 hours or overnight)**
1 medium potato, boiled and mashed
¾ cups carrots, julienned
¾ cup cabbage, shredded
¼ cup bulb of spring onion, chopped finely
¼ cup greens of spring onion, chopped finely
2 garlic cloves, chopped finely
1 tbsp ginger–green chilli paste
1 tsp *chaat masala*
1 tsp dry mango powder
3 tbsp salsa sauce (see recipe on p. 239)
2 tbsp oil
Salt as per taste

METHOD
1. Pressure-cook the soaked chickpeas with ½ tsp salt and 3 cups water for 6–7 whistles. Drain and keep aside.

2. To make the kebab mix, combine the boiled chickpeas, potato, *chaat masala*, dry mango powder and salt as per taste. Refrigerate for half an hour.

3. Meanwhile, to make the veggie mix, heat 1 tbsp oil in a pan, add the bulbs and greens of spring onions, cabbage, carrots and salt. Sauté for 2 minutes. Remove from heat and keep aside.

4. Take out the kebab mix from the refrigerator and divide it into six equal portions. Shape each portion into cylindrical kebabs. Slightly roast each kebab on a non-stick pan with ½ tbsp oil till it turns golden brown on both sides. Keep aside.

5. To make the roll, warm the basic wrap and spread ½ tbsp salsa sauce over it.

6. Then spread ⅓ cup of the veggie mix in the centre of the basic wrap, place the kebab over the veggie mix and roll up tightly.

7. Wrap the roll in foil to keep it hot.

Complete your plate — with a glass of buttermilk.

VALUE PER SERVING (2 ROLLS)

Calories	356 kcal
Protein	10 gm
Fat	10 gm
Carbohydrates	54 gm
Calcium	150 mg
Fibre	2 gm
Iron	3 mg

Chinese Idli Sauté

Semolina idlis sautéed with vegetables and seasoned with a Chinese flavour.

MAKES: 5 cups
SERVING SIZE: 2 cups

PRE-PREPARATION TIME: 30 mins
PREPARATION TIME: 10 mins
COOKING TIME: 20 mins

INGREDIENTS
¾ cup semolina
½ cup fresh curd
1 cup bean sprouts
1 cup cabbage, shredded
½ cup carrots, julienned
½ cup yellow bell pepper, julienned
½ cup French beans, thinly sliced diagonally
2 bulbs of spring onion, sliced thinly
½ cup stalks and greens of spring onion, chopped finely
3–4 garlic cloves, chopped finely
1 tbsp vinegar
2 tbsp Pad Thai sauce
½ tsp powdered sugar
1 tsp Eno fruit salt
3 tbsp oil
Salt as per taste

METHOD

1. **Pre-prep:** Combine the semolina, curd and 2 tbsp water and keep aside for half an hour.
2. Boil 2 cups water in a pan and cook the bean sprouts for 3–4 minutes. Drain and keep aside.
3. Grease two plates of *idli* maker with 1 tbsp oil.
4. Pour water into the *idli* maker and bring to a boil.
5. Meanwhile, to the semolina batter, add sugar and salt as per taste and mix well.
6. When the water in the *idli* maker starts boiling; add Eno fruit salt to the semolina batter, stirring continuously for 10–15 seconds.
7. Immediately pour the semolina batter into the greased plates. Cover and steam for 15 minutes. Remove the plates and allow to cool.
8. Meanwhile, heat 2 tbsp oil in a pan and sauté the garlic. Add the bulbs of spring onions; sauté for a minute.
9. Combine the bell pepper, carrots, French beans and salt; sauté for a minute.
10. Add cabbage, bean sprouts, the greens and stalks of spring onions; sauté for 1–2 minutes.
11. Remove from flame. Add vinegar and Pad Thai sauce. Adjust salt as per taste.
12. Cut each *idli* into eight parts. Combine with the veggie mix. Serve hot!

It's a complete plate!

VALUE PER SERVING (2 CUPS)

Calories	339 kcal
Protein	8 gm
Fat	12 gm
Carbohydrates	49 gm
Fibre	1 gm
Calcium	105 mg
Iron	2 mg

Chipotle Roll

A nutritious roll with Mexican flavoured kidney beans topped with crunchy veggies.

MAKES: 6
SERVING SIZE: 2

PRE-PREPARATION TIME: 6–8 hrs
PREPARATION TIME: 20 mins
COOKING TIME: 30 mins

INGREDIENTS
6 basic wraps (see recipe on p. 235)
¾ cup uncooked kidney beans **(Pre-prep: Soak for 6–8 hours)**
1 large tomato, chopped finely
1 large onion, chopped finely
½ large red bell pepper, julienned
½ large yellow bell pepper, julienned
¾ cup carrots, julienned
½ cup cabbage, shredded
3 garlic cloves, chopped finely
1-inch piece of ginger, julienned
2 dry red chillies
½ tsp dried oregano
1 tbsp mixed dried herbs (Mexican seasoning)
3 tbsp salsa sauce (see recipe on p. 239)
½ tsp black pepper powder
2 tbsp oil
Salt as per taste

METHOD

1. Pressure-cook the kidney beans with the dry red chillies and 3 cups water for 10–12 whistles. (*The kidney beans should be slightly over-cooked.*) Drain and discard the chillies, then cool and mash the beans lightly.
2. Heat 1 tbsp oil in a pan; sauté the garlic and ginger.
3. Add onions; sauté until translucent.
4. Add tomatoes; cook for 5 minutes.
5. Add the mashed kidney beans, mixed dried herbs and salt; sauté for 3 minutes.
6. Add salsa sauce and cook till the beans mix dries completely. Remove from heat and keep aside.
7. Heat 1 tbsp oil in a separate flat pan. Toss in the carrots and bell peppers; sauté for 4–5 minutes.
8. Add cabbage, black pepper powder and salt; sauté for 3 minutes. Remove from heat.
9. Divide the veggie mix into six equal portions and keep aside.
10. To make the roll, warm a basic wrap, spread ⅓ cup of the beans mix on each basic wrap and then spread one portion of the veggie mix and roll it up tightly.
11. Wrap the roll in foil to keep it hot.

It's a complete plate!

VALUE PER SERVING (2 ROLLS)

Calories	435 kcal	Protein	16 gm
Fat	14 gm	Carbohydrates	62 gm
Fibre	2 gm	Calcium	152 mg
Iron	4 mg		

Italian Egg Roll

A wholesome roll to get your fix of eggs and veggies.

MAKES: 6
SERVING SIZE: 2

PREPARATION TIME: 10 mins
COOKING TIME: 20 mins

INGREDIENTS
6 basic wraps (see recipe on p. 235)
2 eggs
5 egg whites
2 cups cabbage, shredded
1 large onion, sliced thinly
¾ cup mushrooms, chopped finely
⅓ cup red bell pepper, chopped finely
1 medium head of broccoli (75 gm), separated into tiny florets
2 bulbs of spring onion, chopped finely
½ cup greens and stalks of spring onion, sliced thinly
3 tbsp fresh basil leaves, chopped finely
3 green chillies, chopped finely
4–5 garlic cloves, chopped finely
3 tbsp cheese, grated
2 tbsp toned milk
1 tsp dried oregano
½ tsp red chilli flakes
¼ tsp black pepper powder
2 tbsp oil
Salt as per taste

METHOD

1. Bring 2 cups water to boil in a pan. Add broccoli and cook for 3 minutes until just tender. Drain and keep aside. When cooled, chop finely.
2. In a bowl, combine the 2 eggs with yolk, 5 egg whites, cheese, milk and salt. Churn with a hand blender to mix completely. Keep aside.
3. Heat 1 tsp oil in a pan. Sauté the onions, cabbage and green chillies for 3-4 minutes. Remove the veggie mix from the heat and keep aside.
4. Heat the remaining 1 tsp oil in a large non-stick flat pan. Sauté the garlic and bulbs of spring onions for 1 minute.
5. Add the bell peppers; sauté for 1 minute.
6. Add the mushrooms, stalks and greens of spring onions and ½ tsp salt; sauté for 2 minutes.
7. Add broccoli; sauté for another minute.
8. Add basil leaves, oregano, chilli flakes, black pepper powder and salt; sauté for 1 minute.
9. Add the beaten egg mix; keep stirring.
10. Keep scraping the bottom frequently with a flexible rubber spatula until the egg mix crumbles. Continue stirring for about 2 minutes, then remove from the flame.
11. To make the roll, warm a basic wrap and first spread a layer of tomato ketchup (optional) on it. Spread ⅓ cup of the egg mix in the centre of each basic wrap. Finally, spread ⅓ cup of the veggie mix over it and roll up tightly.
12. Wrap the roll in foil to keep it hot.

It's a complete plate!

VALUE PER SERVING (2 ROLLS)

Calories	383 kcal
Protein	19 gm
Fat	16 gm
Carbohydrates	39 gm
Fibre	2 gm
Calcium	233 mg
Iron	3 mg

Peas and Cheese Paratha

Goodness of peas and the taste of cheese stuffed in a paratha.

MAKES: 12
SERVING SIZE: 2

PREPARATION TIME: 10 mins
COOKING TIME: 25 mins

INGREDIENTS
FOR THE DOUGH:
3 cups wholewheat flour
½ tsp salt
2 tsp oil (to add to the dough)
6 tsp oil (for roasting the *parathas*)

FOR THE FILLING:
1½ cups green peas, shelled
¾ cup cabbage, chopped finely
1 large potato, boiled, peeled and grated
5 green chillies, chopped finely
2 tbsp ginger, chopped finely
½ tsp dry mango powder
2 tbsp fresh coriander leaves, chopped finely
2 tbsp cheese, grated
1 tbsp oil
Salt as per taste

METHOD

FOR THE FILLING:

1. Rinse the peas in running water and drain. Place the peas, green chillies and ginger in a mixer and grind to a smooth paste, without adding any water.
2. Heat the oil in a non-stick pan. Sauté the peas paste for 3 minutes.
3. Combine cabbage and salt; sauté for another 3–4 minutes.
4. Combine the potato and dry mango powder to the above mix; sauté for another 2 minutes. Remove from heat.
5. Add coriander leaves and cheese; mix well. Set aside to cool.
6. Divide the filling into twelve equal portions; shape each portion into a ball.

FOR THE PARATHAS:

1. Combine the wheat flour, water, salt and 2 tsp oil and knead into a soft dough.
2. Divide the dough into twelve equal portions.
3. Roll a portion of the dough into a 3-inch-diameter disc.
4. Place one portion of the filling in the centre of the disc. Bring together all the sides to the centre and seal tightly.
5. Roll again into a 5-inch-diameter disc with a little flour.
6. Heat a *tava* and cook each *paratha* using ½ tsp oil. Roast on both sides until golden brown. Serve with pickle.

Complete your plate—with a bowl of curd or flavoured yoghurt.

VALUE PER SERVING (2 PARATHAS)

Calories	301 kcal
Protein	9 gm
Fat	9 gm
Carbohydrates	46 gm
Fibre	2 gm
Calcium	196 mg
Iron	3 mg

Potato and Chickpea Roll

A satiating roll packed with energy and power.

MAKES: 12
SERVING SIZE: 2

PRE-PREPARATION TIME: 6–8 hours
PREPARATION TIME: 20 mins
COOKING TIME: 20 mins

INGREDIENTS
12 basic wraps (see recipe on p. 235)
1 cup uncooked chickpeas **(Pre-prep: Soak for 6–8 hours or overnight)**
2 large potatoes, boiled, peeled and diced into tiny cubes
2 large onions, chopped finely
2 large tomatoes, chopped finely
6 garlic cloves, grated finely
1-inch piece of ginger, grated finely
4 tbsp fresh coriander leaves, chopped finely
1 tsp red chilli powder
½ tsp turmeric powder
2 tsp dry mango powder
2 tsp *chhole masala*
2 tbsp oil
Salt as per taste

METHOD
1. Pressure-cook the chickpeas with 1 tsp salt and 4 cups of water for 8 whistles. Drain, cool and mash lightly. Keep aside.

2. Heat oil in a pan; sauté the garlic and ginger.
3. Add onions; sauté until translucent.
4. Add turmeric powder, chilli powder and *chhole masala*; sauté for a few seconds.
5. Add tomatoes; sauté for another minute.
6. Cook the mix on a low flame for a further 4–5 minutes.
7. Add potatoes, chickpeas, dry mango powder, coriander leaves and salt; sauté for another 2 minutes. Remove from heat.
8. To make the roll, warm a basic wrap. Spread ⅓ cup of the chickpea mix in the centre of the wrap and roll up tightly.
9. Wrap the roll in foil to keep it hot.

It's a complete plate!

VALUE PER SERVING (2 ROLLS)	
Calories	378 kcal
Protein	10 gm
Fat	11 gm
Carbohydrates	58 gm
Fibre	2 gm
Calcium	156 mg
Iron	4 mg

Ragi Veggie Uttapam

Brownie with Cream Cheese

Chana Kebab Roll

Chinese Idli Sauté

Corn and Spinach Toast

Creamy Corn Crackers/Pancakes

Creamy Corn Crackers/Pancakes

Creamy Egg Toast

Flavoured Yoghurt Shots

Jello on Banoffee

Mini Paneer Pizza

Mini Sliders

Minty Fruity Cooler

Mushroom Risotto

Nachos Bhel

Quick Pineapple Soufflé

Spinach and Paneer Roll

Spinach Masala Dosa

Spinach and Spaghetti Bake

Sweet and Sour Dragon Roll

Sweet and Sour Veg Chow Mein

Vegetable Hot Dog

Zucchini and Mushroom Sandwich

Tangy Bean Curry
with Green Leafy Paratha

Spinach and Paneer Roll

Cottage cheese wrapped into a roll with the nutrition of spinach and crunch of cabbage.

MAKES: 10
SERVING SIZE: 2

PREPARATION TIME: 20 mins
COOKING TIME: 20 mins

INGREDIENTS
10 basic wraps (see recipe on p. 235)
200 gm paneer (see recipe on p. 237)
2 large onions, chopped finely
4 cups spinach, chopped finely
2 cups cabbage, shredded
2 green chillies, chopped finely
6 garlic cloves, grated
1 tsp red chilli powder
3 tbsp hot and sweet tomato ketchup
1½ tbsp oil
Salt as per taste

METHOD
1. Mix ¼ tsp salt with the chopped spinach and keep aside for 10 minutes.
2. Grate the paneer into thick shreds. Keep aside.
3. Squeeze out all the excess water from the spinach. Keep aside.
4. Heat oil in a pan. Sauté the garlic and green chillies.

5. Add onions; sauté until translucent.
6. Add red chilli powder; sauté for 1 minute.
7. Add spinach; sauté for 4 minutes.
8. Add cabbage and salt as per taste; sauté for 5 minutes.
9. Combine the grated paneer and remove from heat.
10. Add the hot and sweet tomato ketchup. Mix well.
11. To make the rolls, warm a basic wrap on a non-stick pan. Spread ⅓ cup of the mix in the centre of the wrap and roll up tightly.
12 Wrap the roll in foil to keep it hot.

It's a complete plate!

VALUE PER SERVING (2 ROLLS)

Calories	404 kcal
Protein	14 gm
Fat	19 gm
Carbohydrates	37 gm
Fibre	1 gm
Calcium	508 mg
Iron	2 mg

Sweet and Sour Dragon Roll

Tangy Schezwan noodles wrapped in a roll.

MAKES: 10
SERVING SIZE: 2

PREPARATION TIME: 10 mins
COOKING TIME: 20 mins

INGREDIENTS
10 basic wraps (see recipe on p. 235)
⅓ packet (50 gm) hakka noodles, uncooked
75 gm paneer (see recipe on p. 237)
1 cup bean sprouts
¾ cup cabbage, shredded
½ cup carrots, julienned
½ cup French beans, sliced diagonally
½ cup red bell peppers, julienned
2 bulbs of spring onions, chopped finely
½ cup stalks and greens of spring onions, chopped finely
4 garlic cloves, chopped finely
1-inch piece of ginger, julienned
1 tbsp vinegar
1 tsp soya sauce
1 ½ tbsp Schezwan sauce
2 tbsp hot and sweet tomato ketchup
2 tbsp oil
Salt as per taste

METHOD

1. Boil water in a pan. Drop the noodles in boiling water and cook for 5 minutes or till done.
2. Drain and wash the boiled noodles under running water. Spread on a flat surface and toss in ½ tsp oil to prevent sticking. Keep aside.
3. Cut the paneer into thin strips. Keep aside.
4. Heat the rest of the oil in a wok; sauté the ginger and garlic for 5–10 seconds.
5. Add bulbs of spring onions; sauté until translucent.
6. Add carrots and French beans; sauté for 3 minutes.
7. Add the greens and stalks of spring onions along with bell peppers and cabbage; sauté for 4–5 minutes.
8. Add vinegar, soya sauce and salt; sauté for a minute.
9. Add the hot and sweet tomato ketchup and Schezwan sauce; sauté for another minute.
10. Combine the noodles to the above and mix well.
11. Combine the paneer and toss lightly. Remove from heat.
12. To make the roll, warm a basic wrap. Spread ⅓ cup of the noodle mix in the centre of the wrap and roll it up tightly.
13. Wrap the roll in foil to keep it hot.

It's a complete plate!

VALUE PER SERVING (2 ROLLS)

Calories	353 kcal	Protein	9 gm
Fat	15 gm	Carbohydrates	43 gm
Fibre	1 gm	Calcium	230 mg
Iron	2 mg		

Snacks

Introduction

Gone are the days when *chivda*, *chakli* and chips made for typical snacks. Kids these days are not satisfied with just biscuits or dry snacks after school and the demand is for stomach-filling and tasty food items. Offering the perfect solution are these yummy, street food snacks made with a twist, an antidote to children going overboard on packaged foods like Maggi and Top Ramen instant noodles. Dishes like Cream Cracker Crunch, Hot Dog Rolls, Vegetable Hakka Noodles in Red Sauce and Paneer Capsicum Tartine are not only quick and easy to prepare but also have great flavours which add variety to daily snacks. Prepare these to avoid your child from bingeing on salty chips and *chakli*s.

Cream Cracker Crunch

A quick mix drenched in white sauce on a crunchy biscuit base.

MAKES: 12
SERVING SIZE: 2

PREPARATION TIME: 10 mins
COOKING TIME: 25 mins

INGREDIENTS
12 cream cracker biscuits
½ cup carrots, chopped finely
½ cup French beans, sliced thinly
¾ cup fresh corn (from cob) or sweet corn kernels
½ cup celery stalk, chopped finely
¾ cup cold toned milk
1 tbsp cornflour
½ tsp powdered sugar
1½ tbsp hot and sweet tomato ketchup
½ tsp black pepper powder
2 tbsp butter
Salt as per taste

METHOD
1. Pressure-cook the sweet corn in 2 cups of water for 4 whistles. Drain and keep aside.
2. Boil the carrots and French beans in 2–3 cups of water for 5–7 minutes. Let them cool, then squeeze out the water completely and keep aside.
3. To make the white sauce, boil ½ cup milk in a pan.
4. Dissolve the cornflour in the remaining ¼ cup cold

milk, and stir till dissolved completely. Add this to the boiling milk and stir constantly to prevent lumps from forming.

5. When the mixture reaches a semi-thick consistency, add ¼ tsp black pepper powder, sugar and salt as per taste. Remove from heat and set aside.

6. Heat butter in a non-stick pan. Add the celery stalk, remaining black pepper powder and salt. Cook on a low flame for 1–2 minutes.

7. Add the boiled corn, carrot and French beans; sauté for a minute.

8. Add the white sauce to the above and stir well.

9. Remove from heat. Stir in the hot and sweet tomato ketchup.

10. Put 1½ tbsp of the mix on each cream cracker biscuit.

12. Cut each cracker into two triangles with a knife/pizza cutter and serve.

Complete your plate—with a glass of milk.

VALUE PER SERVING (2 CRACKERS)

Calories	118 kcal
Protein	3 gm
Fat	3 gm
Carbohydrates	19 gm
Fibre	1 gm
Calcium	52 mg
Iron	0.5 mg

Crisp Alfredo Toast

Colourful vegetables drenched in white sauce, spread over a slice of bread and baked to crispy perfection.

MAKES: 6
SERVING SIZE: 2

PREPARATION TIME: 10 mins
COOKING TIME: 25 mins

INGREDIENTS
6 slices white/wholewheat bread
½ cup toned milk
1 medium onion, chopped finely
1 cup mushrooms, chopped finely
¼ cup carrots, chopped finely
¼ cup capsicum, chopped finely
¼ cup baby corn, chopped finely
¼ cup cabbage, chopped finely
¼ cup tiny broccoli florets
2 garlic cloves, chopped finely
2 tbsp mayonnaise
35 gm cheese, grated
1 tbsp cornflour
1 tsp red chilli flakes
½ tsp dried oregano
1 tbsp olive oil
Salt as per taste

METHOD

1. Preheat the oven at 160° C for 7–10 minutes.
2. Heat oil in a pan. Add the garlic and sauté for a few seconds.
3. Add onions and capsicum; sauté for 3–4 minutes.
4. Add cabbage, carrots, baby corn, broccoli, mushrooms and ½ tsp salt; sauté for 5–7 minutes.
5. Add ¼ cup milk to the above and cook for 1–2 minutes.
6. Meanwhile, dissolve cornflour in the remaining ¼ cup cold milk and stir till dissolved completely. Add it to the above preparation and add salt as per taste.
7. Add mayonnaise and grated cheese; cook until the mixture thickens.
8. Finally, add dried oregano and red chilli flakes. Remove from heat.
9. Lightly toast the bread slices in a toaster or the preheated oven for 2–3 minutes.
10. Divide the mixture into six equal portions. Spread each portion on each toast and bake in the preheated oven for 8–10 minutes.

Complete your plate — with a glass of milk.

VALUE PER SERVING (2 TOASTS)

Calories	290 kcal	Protein	9 gm
Fat	14 gm	Carbohydrates	31 gm
Fibre	1 gm	Calcium	212 mg
Iron	2 mg		

Mini Paneer Pizzas

Kids' favourite pizzas, made from paneer instead of melted cheese.

MAKES: 8
SERVING SIZE: 2

PREPARATION TIME: 10 mins
COOKING TIME: 25 mins

INGREDIENTS

8 mini pizza bases
70 gm paneer (see recipe on p. 237)
5 large tomatoes
1 large onion, chopped finely
½ cup red and yellow bell peppers, chopped finely
6–8 garlic cloves, chopped finely
2 tbsp fresh basil leaves, chopped finely
2 tbsp tomato ketchup
½ tsp red chilli powder
½ tsp black pepper powder
35 gm cheese, grated (optional)
Juice of 1½ lemons
4 tsp butter
1 tbsp olive oil
Salt as per taste

METHOD

1. Preheat the oven at 160° C for 7–10 minutes.
2. Grate the paneer and keep it aside.
3. Drop the tomatoes in a pan of boiling water for 7–8 minutes. Drain (reserve the stock) and cool.

4. Peel the blanched tomatoes and chop them coarsely. Keep aside.
5. Heat oil in a pan; sauté the garlic for a few seconds.
6. Add onions; sauté for 2 minutes.
7. Add bell peppers; sauté for 3–4 minutes.
8. Add tomatoes; cook for another 5 minutes.
9. Add red chilli powder, black pepper powder and salt. Cook for 3–4 minutes.
10. Add ½ cup of the reserved tomato stock. Cook for another 5 minutes.
11. Add basil leaves and ketchup. Cook till the gravy mixture becomes almost dry. Keep aside.
12. Apply a little butter on the underside of each pizza base and place them in the preheated oven for 2–3 minutes.
13. Remove the bases from the oven and spread 2 tbsp of the gravy on each pizza base.
14. Garnish with 1 tbsp grated paneer on each pizza.
15. Return the pizzas to the oven to bake for 5–7 minutes. Serve hot!

Complete your plate—with a fruit.

Variation: One can use chopped, hard-boiled egg whites (from three eggs) as a topping instead of paneer.

VALUE PER SERVING (2 MINI PIZZAS)			
Calories	285 kcal	Protein	9 gm
Fat	9 gm	Carbohydrates	39 gm
Fibre	2 gm	Calcium	242 mg
Iron	1 mg		

Nutri Chaat on Bread

Tangy and nutritious chaat spread on bread.

MAKES: 10
SERVING SIZE: 2

PRE-PREPARATION TIME: 8 hrs
PREPARATION TIME: 10 mins
COOKING TIME: 15 mins

INGREDIENTS
10 slices white/wholewheat bread
¼ cup uncooked green gram **(Pre-prep: Soak for 6–8 hours, drain and keep covered)**
¼ cup small red *chana* **(Pre-prep: Soak for 8 hours, drain and keep covered)**
1 large onion, chopped finely
1 large tomato, chopped finely
1 large potato, boiled, peeled and diced
½ cup cabbage, chopped finely
2 green chillies, chopped finely
3 tbsp date/tamarind chutney
¼ cup fresh coconut, grated
⅓ cup roasted peanuts, crushed coarsely
¼ cup fresh coriander leaves, chopped finely
2 tsp cumin powder
½ tsp red chilli powder
Salt as per taste

FOR GARNISHING:

¼ cup fresh coriander leaves, chopped finely

¼ cup fresh coconut, grated (optional)

¼ cup roasted peanuts, crushed coarsely

¼ cup date/tamarind chutney

METHOD

1. Boil the soaked green gram in water for 7–8 minutes. Drain and keep aside.

2. Rinse the *chana*; pressure-cook with 2 cups of water and a pinch of salt for 3 whistles. Drain and keep aside.

3. Combine all the ingredients in a bowl except those listed for garnishing.

4. On each slice of bread put a few drops of date/tamarind chutney and spread ⅓ cup of the *chaat* mix.

5. Garnish with crushed peanuts, grated fresh coconut and coriander leaves; then cut each bread *chaat* into four squares and serve immediately.

Complete your plate—with a glass of buttermilk.

Variation: You can also choose either green gram or red *chana* if you don't wish to use both. Follow the cooking steps as per the pulse chosen.

VALUE PER SERVING (2 BREAD CHAATS)

Calories	317 kcal	Protein	11 gm
Fat	11 gm	Carbohydrates	45 gm
Fibre	2 gm	Calcium	138 mg
Iron	3 mg		

Paneer Capsicum Tartine

A refreshing evening snack with paneer, capsicum and baby corn.

MAKES: 8
SERVING SIZE: 2

PREPARATION TIME: 5 mins
COOKING TIME: 25 mins

INGREDIENTS
8 slices white/wholewheat bread
125 gm paneer (see recipe on p. 237)
1½ cups cold toned milk
2 cups (150 gm) mushrooms, chopped finely
3 baby corns, sliced thinly
1½ cups spinach, chopped finely
½ cup red bell peppers, chopped finely
2 bulbs of spring onions, chopped finely
¼ cup greens of spring onions, chopped finely
2 green chillies, chopped finely
1½ tbsp cornflour
1 tsp powdered sugar
1 tsp dried oregano
1 tsp red chilli flakes
½ tsp black pepper powder
1 tbsp oil
Salt as per taste

METHOD
1. Preheat the oven at 160° C for 7–10 minutes.

2. Bring 2 cups water to a boil in a pan. Cook the sliced baby corn in it for 7–8 minutes or until tender. Drain and keep aside.
3. Dice the paneer into tiny cubes.
4. To make the white sauce, boil ½ cup milk in a pan.
5. Dissolve cornflour in the remaining 1¼ cup cold milk, and stir till dissolved completely. Add this to the boiling milk and stir constantly to prevent lumps from forming.
6. When it reaches a semi-thick consistency, add ¼ tsp black pepper powder, sugar and salt as per taste. Remove from heat and set aside.
7. Heat oil in a pan. Add the green chillies and bulbs of spring onions and sauté for 1 minute.
8. Add bell peppers; sauté for 2 minutes.
9. Add baby corn and greens of spring onions; sauté for a minute.
10. Add mushrooms; sauté for another minute.
11. Add the paneer to the spinach mix; sauté for a minute.
12. Stir in the white sauce and cook for another minute. Add dried oregano, red chilli flakes and salt as per taste.
13. Use a small cookie cutter (approximately 3-inch diameter) to cut a round of each bread slice (leaving out only the sides).
14. Lightly toast the rounds in the preheated oven for 2–3 minutes.
15. Spread ⅓ cup of the paneer mix on each toasted round and bake in the preheated oven for 3–4 minutes. Serve hot.

VALUE PER SERVING (2 TARTINES)

Calories	301 kcal
Protein	12 gm
Fat	15 gm
Carbohydrates	24 gm
Fibre	1 gm
Calcium	472 mg
Iron	1 mg

Peas and Potato Patties

Peas-filled potato patties.

MAKES: 6
SERVING SIZE: 2

PREPARATION TIME: 10 mins
COOKING TIME: 25 mins

INGREDIENTS
3 medium potatoes
70 gm paneer (see recipe on p. 237)
1 cup peas, shelled
2 slices white bread
2 tbsp fresh coconut, grated
2 green chillies, chopped coarsely
½ tsp cumin powder
Juice of 1 lemon
4 tsp oil
Salt as per taste

METHOD
1. Pressure-cook the potatoes in enough water for 3 whistles. Open immediately and drain.
2. When slightly cooled, peel the potatoes and grate them.
3. Squeeze the paneer and drain the water completely.
4. Coarsely grind the peas in a mixer along with the green chillies.
5. Heat ½ tsp oil in a pan. Cook the pea paste along with cumin powder and salt on a low flame for 8–10 minutes.

6. Remove from heat and add the grated coconut. Mix well and set aside to cool.
7. Divide the pea mix into six equal portions, and shape each portion into a ball. Keep aside. These are the pea balls.
8. Grind the bread slices in a mixer.
9. Now combine the grated potato, bread mixture, paneer, lemon juice and salt as per taste. Mix well.
10. Divide the potato mix into six equal portions, and shape each portion into a ball. Keep aside. These are the potato balls.
11. Take one potato ball and flatten it a bit to form a cup in your palm. Place one pea ball in the centre of the cup and fold in all sides covering the peas ball completely.
12. Flatten it a bit again and shape into a patty. Repeat for the remaining balls.
13. Heat a pan. Roast each patty using ½ tsp oil until it turns golden brown on both sides.
14. Serve with green chutney and/or ketchup.

Complete your plate—with a glass of buttermilk .

VALUE PER SERVING (2 PATTIES)

Calories	310 kcal
Protein	9 gm
Fat	14 gm
Carbohydrates	33 gm
Fibre	2 gm
Calcium	264 mg
Iron	1 mg

Spinach Masala Dosa

Classic Mysore masala dosa filling enveloped in a dosa made of green gram.

MAKES: 10
SERVING SIZE: 2

PRE-PREPARATION TIME: 4 hrs
PREPARATION TIME: 10 mins
COOKING TIME: 20 mins

INGREDIENTS

1 cup uncooked split green gram or yellow gram **(Pre-prep: Soak for 3–4 hours, drain and keep covered)**
2 cups spinach, cleaned
2 large onions, chopped finely
2 large tomatoes, chopped finely
2 large potatoes, boiled, peeled and mashed
1 cup capsicum, chopped finely
½ cup fresh coriander leaves, chopped finely
2 green chillies, chopped finely
1-inch piece of ginger, chopped finely
1½ tbsp *pav bhaji masala*
½ tsp turmeric powder
½ tsp cumin powder
1 tsp red chilli powder
1½ tbsp oil
1½ tbsp butter
Salt as per taste

METHOD

1. Place the spinach in a pan with a little water. Cover and cook for 5–6 minutes or till it wilts completely. Drain and cool. Chop coarsely.
2. Grind the soaked dal, green chillies and ginger in a mixer.
3. Add the chopped spinach and a little water and grind again. Add salt to this batter and keep aside.
4. Heat oil; sauté onions till translucent.
5. Add capsicum and 1 tsp salt; sauté for 1 minute.
6. Add turmeric powder, red chilli powder, cumin powder, *pav bhaji masala* and salt; sauté for another minute.
7. Add the tomatoes; sauté for 2 minutes.
8. Add the mashed potato and coriander leaves; sauté for another minute. Remove the veggie mix from heat and keep aside.
9. Heat a non-stick *dosa tava*; wipe with a damp cloth.
10. Spread ¼ cup of the batter to make a thin *dosa*. Drizzle ½ tsp butter on the sides. Spread ⅓ cup of the veggie mix on the *dosa*. Cook till the underside is golden and crisp.
11. Gently lift from one side with a spatula and fold over to make a roll.
12. Cut into three big pieces and serve with coconut chutney and/or ketchup.
13. Repeat for the remaining dosas.

Complete your plate—with a glass of buttermilk.

VALUE PER SERVING (2 DOSAS)

Calories	263 kcal
Protein	11 gm
Fat	7 gm
Carbohydrates	39 gm
Fibre	2 gm
Calcium	100 mg
Iron	2 mg

Steamed Vegetable Seekh Kebabs

Wholesome snack with a combination of flours, veggies and fresh greens.

MAKES: 30
SERVING SIZE: 6

PREPARATION TIME: 10 mins
COOKING TIME: 15 mins

INGREDIENTS
½ cup wholewheat flour
½ cup pearl millet flour
½ cup gram flour (*besan*)
1 cup bottle gourd, grated finely
½ cup carrot, grated finely
½ cup spinach, chopped finely
½ cup fenugreek leaves, chopped finely
1 tbsp ginger–green chilli paste
Juice of 1 lemon
1 tbsp powdered sugar
½ tsp red chilli powder
¼ tsp asafoetida
½ tsp turmeric powder
½ tsp cumin powder
½ tsp Eno fruit salt
½ tbsp oil
Salt as per taste
2 tbsp fresh coriander leaves, chopped finely (for garnishing)

FOR TEMPERING:

½ tsp mustard seeds
1 tsp white sesame seeds
8–10 curry leaves
2–3 green chillies, slit into halves
1 tbsp oil

METHOD

1. Combine the spinach and fenugreek leaves. Add ½ tsp salt and mix well. Keep aside for 5 minutes. Then squeeze out all the liquid.
2. Similarly, sprinkle the bottle gourd with salt, keep aside for 5 minutes and then squeeze out all the liquid. Retain this liquid.
3. Boil some water in a steamer/*dhokla*-maker.
4. Meanwhile, combine all three flours, bottle gourd, carrot, spinach, fenugreek, ginger–green chilli paste, red chilli powder, cumin powder, powdered sugar, turmeric and asafoetida along with ½ tbsp oil, salt, fruit salt, lemon juice and 1–2 tbsp of the liquid retained from the bottle gourd. Knead into a soft dough.
5. Divide the dough into four equal parts and make long cylindrical rolls from each part (about 6 inches in length and 1½ inches in diameter). Coat each roll with a little oil.
6. The minute the water starts boiling in the steamer/*dhokla*-maker, arrange the four rolls on a greased, hole-bottomed tray. Let the rolls steam in the steamer/*dhokla*-maker for about 25 minutes.
7. Remove the tray from the steamer/*dhokla*-maker and let the rolls cool for about 5–7 minutes.

8. Then cut each roll diagonally into 7–8 small kebabs.
9. For tempering, heat 1 tbsp oil in a wide pan; add mustard seeds. When the seeds crackle, add sesame seeds, curry leaves and green chillies. Add the sliced kebabs and lightly sauté them for about 2–3 minutes. Garnish with coriander leaves.

Complete your plate—with a glass of buttermilk.

VALUE PER SERVING (6 KEBABS)

Calories	175 kcal
Protein	5 gm
Fat	5 gm
Carbohydrates	26 gm
Fibre	1 gm
Calcium	112 mg
Iron	3 mg

Vegetable Hakka Noodles in Red Sauce

A healthier replacement for instant noodles like Maggi and Top Ramen.

MAKES: 6 cups
SERVING SIZE: 1 cup

PREPARATION TIME: 10 mins
COOKING TIME: 20 mins

INGREDIENTS
⅔ packet (100 gm) hakka noodles, uncooked
6 large tomatoes
1 cup cabbage, shredded
1 cup carrots, julienned
1 cup French beans, sliced diagonally
2 medium onions, sliced finely
½ cup greens of spring onion, chopped finely
2 tbsp ginger–green chilli paste
2 tbsp hot and sweet tomato ketchup
3 tbsp oil
Salt as per taste

METHOD
1. Boil water in a pan. Drop the noodles and boil for 10–12 minutes or till the noodles are cooked.
2. Drain and wash the boiled noodles under running water. Spread on a flat surface and toss in ½ tsp oil to prevent sticking. Keep aside.

3. Put the tomatoes in another pan of boiling water for 7–8 minutes. Drain and cool.
4. Peel the blanched tomatoes and grind them in a mixer. Sieve the puree and keep aside.
5. Heat oil in a wok; sauté the ginger–green chilli paste.
6. Add onions; sauté for a minute.
7. Add carrots, French beans and salt; cook for 5–7 minutes.
8. Add cabbage and greens of spring onions; cook for 3–4 minutes.
9. Meanwhile, boil the tomato puree in a separate pan. Add black pepper powder.
10. Add this tomato puree to the vegetable mix.
11. Add ½ cup water and salt as per taste; cook for another 3–4 minutes.
12. Add hot and sweet tomato ketchup. Add the noodles and serve hot.

Tip: Adding boiled, chopped egg whites to the noodles will improve the protein content of the dish.

VALUE PER SERVING (1 CUP)

Calories	166 kcal
Protein	4 gm
Fat	6 gm
Carbohydrates	24 gm
Fibre	1 gm
Calcium	77 mg
Iron	1 mg

Vegetable Hot Dog

Tangy vegetable mix filled in hot dog rolls, ready to be had 'on the go'!

MAKES: 4
SERVING SIZE: 1

PREPARATION TIME: 10 mins
COOKING TIME: 15 mins

INGREDIENTS
4 hot dog rolls (5-inch)
1 cup toned milk
1 cup bean sprouts
1 medium onion, chopped finely
1 medium capsicum, chopped finely
½ large red bell pepper, chopped finely
½ large yellow bell pepper, chopped finely
¾ cup cabbage, chopped finely
¼ cup fresh basil leaves, chopped finely
4 tbsp pizza/pasta sauce
1 tsp red chilli flakes
1 tsp dried oregano
1 tbsp cornflour
¼ tsp black pepper powder
1 tbsp butter
1 tbsp oil
Salt as per taste
½ cup greens of spring onions, chopped finely (for garnishing)

METHOD

1. Boil water and cook the bean sprouts in it for 4 minutes. Drain and cool.
2. Heat oil. Add onions and sauté until translucent.
3. Add the capsicum and bell peppers; sauté for 2 minutes.
4. Add cabbage, bean sprouts, black pepper powder and salt; sauté for a minute.
5. Add basil leaves, dried oregano and red chilli flakes; sauté for another minute.
6. Mix in the cornflour with the cold milk and add to above preparation. Keep stirring till the mixture thickens.
7. Adjust seasonings as per taste. Keep aside to cool.
8. Divide the mixture into four equal portions.
9. To serve, butter the outer sides of the hot dog rolls and warm the rolls on the *tava*. Then slit each roll vertically (but not completely).
10. Spread pizza/pasta sauce on the inner sides of the top and bottom of the rolls.
11. Put one portion of the mixture on the bottom half of each roll and garnish with spring onion greens.
12. Close with the top half of the hot dog roll. It's ready to serve.

Complete your plate—with a glass of buttermilk.

VARIATION:

1. Scoop out the bread to reduce the carbohydrate content and add more vegetable mixture.
2. You can also toast the hot dogs in a preheated oven instead of on a *tava*.

VALUE PER SERVING (1 ROLL)

Calories	444 kcal
Protein	13 gm
Fat	14 gm
Carbohydrates	66 gm
Fibre	1 gm
Calcium	92 mg
Iron	0.5 mg

Dinner

Introduction

Indian meals were conventionally had sitting on the floor (the posture is said to aid digestion), and would include dal, *roti* and *sabzi*. Today, however, dinners are eaten parked in front of television sets and in bedrooms, and mostly constitute food low in protein, like pasta, pizza, noodles, sandwiches, *pav bhaji*, etc. Dinner proteins are of utmost importance as they prevent midnight hunger pangs and help avoid late-night snacking. A wholesome dinner has the right combination of carbohydrates, protein and fats along with sufficient fibre content. The recipes here are ideal for scrummy family meals for your children, and the ingredients have been chosen so as to aid sound sleep and healthy growth, as well as boost immunity.

Chhole with Potato Tikki

Potato and cauliflower tikkis served with chickpeas makes for a tasty and wholesome meal.

MAKES: 6 cups chhole and 12 tikkis
SERVING SIZE: 1 cup chhole with 2 tikkis

PRE-PREPARATION TIME: 6–8 hrs
PREPARATION TIME: 30 mins
COOKING TIME: 42 mins

INGREDIENTS
FOR THE CHHOLE:
1 cup uncooked chickpeas* **(Pre-prep: Soak for 6–8 hours or overnight)**
3 medium onions, chopped coarsely
1 medium tomato, chopped coarsely
3 green chillies, chopped coarsely
1-inch piece of ginger, chopped coarsely
5 garlic cloves, chopped coarsely
6–8 black peppercorns
2 big cardamoms, deskinned
3 cloves
1 tsp cumin seeds
1½ tbsp dried pomegranate seeds (*anardana*)
2–3 bay leaves
1 cinnamon stick
3 tbsp tea leaves, tied in a muslin cloth (optional)

---

* Instead of using 1 cup uncooked chickpeas, you can also use 2 cups canned garbanzo beans. No need to pressure-cook them.

2 tbsp oil
Salt as per taste
Fresh coriander leaves (for garnishing)

FOR THE TIKKIS:
2 slices white bread
4 cups cauliflower, separated into small florets
2 medium potatoes, boiled, peeled and mashed
2 tbsp oil
Salt as per taste

METHOD
FOR THE CHHOLE:
1. Soak the pomegranate seeds in ½ cup water for 30 minutes and keep aside.
2. Meanwhile, drain and rinse the soaked chickpeas, and pressure-cook them with the tea leaves, 1 tsp salt and 5 cups water for 8–10 whistles. Then, retain the cooked chickpeas with the leftover water; discard the tea leaves.
3. In a broad non-stick pan, dry-roast the bay leaves, cumin seeds, black peppercorns, cinnamon stick and cardamoms for about 2 minutes. Set aside to cool.
4. In a mixer, grind the onions and keep aside.
5. Then grind the dry-roasted spices along with tomato, green chillies, ginger and garlic. Keep aside.
6. Heat 3 tbsp oil in a heavy bottom or iron wok. Sauté the onion paste till it becomes dark brown in colour. This will take about 15 minutes.
7. Meanwhile, grind the soaked pomegranate seeds in a mixer with water. After it turns into a paste, sieve

through a strainer and reserve the water. This is the *anardana* water.

8. Then add the tomato paste to the cooked onion paste and let it cook for 10 minutes.
9. Combine the boiled chickpeas along with the water it was cooked in. Let it cook for another 10 minutes.
10. Add the *anardana* water.
11. Add salt as per taste and cook for another 5–7 minutes. Remove from heat and set aside.

FOR THE TIKKIS:
1. Boil the cauliflower florets until tender. Drain and squeeze out all the excess water. Mash along with boiled potatoes.
2. Grind the bread slices in a mixer. Add to the cauliflower–potato mixture along with salt as per taste.
3. Divide into twelve portions and roll into balls. Flatten each ball to make a patty. Shallow-fry all the patties in a non-stick pan using 2 tbsp oil till they turn golden brown on both sides.

TO SERVE:
1. Spread 1 cup cooked chickpeas on two patties and garnish with coriander leaves.
2. If desired, drizzle some tamarind chutney and coriander chutney.

Complete your plate—with a glass of buttermilk or a bowl of curd.

VALUE PER SERVING (1 CUP CHHOLE WITH 2 TIKKIS)

Calories	285 kcal
Protein	8 gm
Fat	9 gm
Carbohydrates	34 gm
Fibre	2 gm
Calcium	107 mg
Iron	3 mg

Mexican Rice with Beans and Corn

A complete and colourful meal, sure to appeal!

MAKES: 5 cups
SERVING SIZE: 2 cups

PREPARATION TIME: 15 mins
COOKING TIME: 20 mins

INGREDIENTS
¾ cup rice, uncooked
1 cup canned baked beans
½ cup fresh corn (from cob) or sweet corn kernels
½ cup red bell peppers, chopped finely
½ cup yellow bell peppers, chopped finely
½ cup cabbage, chopped finely
1 large bulb of spring onion, chopped finely
¼ cup stalk of spring onion, chopped finely
¼ cup greens of spring onion, chopped finely
2 tbsp salsa sauce (see recipe on p. 239)
1 tsp mixed dried herbs (Mexican seasoning)
2 tbsp olive oil
Salt as per taste

METHOD
1. Bring 4½ cups water to a boil.
2. Rinse the rice thoroughly and add to the boiling water.
3. Cook for 10 minutes or till the rice is cooked *al dente* (not too soft). Drain and spread it in a wide pan to cool.

4. Pressure-cook the sweet corn with 1 cup water for 3–4 whistles. Drain and keep aside.
5. Heat the oil in a large wok. Add the bulbs of spring onions; sauté until translucent.
6. Add the bell peppers; sauté for 2 minutes.
7. Add the boiled corn, stalks of spring onions, cabbage and a pinch of salt; sauté for a minute.
8. Add the baked beans, greens of spring onions and dried mixed herbs; sauté for another minute.
9. Stir in the salsa sauce.
10. Finally, add the cooked rice and sprinkle salt as per taste. Remove from heat and serve hot.

It's a complete plate!

VALUE PER SERVING (2 CUPS)	
Calories	379 kcal
Protein	12 gm
Fat	11 gm
Carbohydrates	35 gm
Fibre	4 gm
Calcium	76 mg
Iron	4 mg

Mushroom Risotto

Mushroom risotto cooked in a tangy tomato puree and blended with white sauce.

MAKES: 6 cups
SERVING SIZE: 1½ cups

PREPARATION TIME: 10 mins
COOKING TIME: 50 mins

INGREDIENTS
1 cup Arborio rice, uncooked (or any other short-grained rice)
2 cups cold toned milk
1½ cups mushrooms, sliced
1 large onion, chopped finely
4 medium tomatoes
½ cup red and yellow bell peppers, chopped finely
6–8 garlic cloves, chopped finely
2 tbsp fresh basil leaves, chopped finely
4 cups vegetable stock (made from 1 cube)
2 tsp cornflour
1 tsp powdered sugar
1 tsp black pepper powder
2 tbsp butter
Salt as per taste
2 tbsp cheese, grated (optional; for garnishing)
Mixed dried herbs (Italian seasoning) as per taste (for garnishing)
Red chilli flakes as per taste (for garnishing)

METHOD

1. Drop the tomatoes in a pan of boiling water for 7–8 minutes. Drain and cool.
2. Remove the skin and grind them in a mixer. Sieve the puree and keep aside.
3. Boil the vegetable stock and store it in a flask so that it remains hot.
4. Heat butter in a large non-stick pan (preferably one with a transparent lid).
5. Sauté the garlic until fragrant.
6. Add onions; sauté until translucent.
7. Add bell peppers; sauté for a minute.
8. Add mushrooms; sauté for another minute.
9. Add the rice, tomato puree and 1 tsp salt; cover with the lid and let it cook.
10. When the puree starts drying up, add ½ cup of vegetable stock. Cover and let it simmer.
11. After 5–7 minutes or when the stock has almost dried, add ½ cup stock. Cover and let it cook further. Repeat this till you add 2 more cups of the stock, ½ cup at a time.
12. Add a total of 3 cups stock as above, ½ cup at a time. Let the rice continue to simmer.
13. Meanwhile, to make the white sauce, boil 1½ cups milk in a pan.
14. Dissolve cornflour in the remaining ½ cup cold milk, and stir till dissolved completely. Add it to the boiling milk and stir constantly to prevent lumps from forming.
15. When the sauce reaches a semi-thick consistency, add ½ tsp black pepper powder, sugar and salt as per taste. Remove from heat and set aside.

16. Check the rice again. If the stock has dried up, add another ½ cup stock and half of the basil leaves. Cover and cook.
17. Repeat for the remaining basil leaves and ½ cup stock. Season with salt and black pepper powder as per taste.
18. Lastly, combine the white sauce.
19. Garnish with grated cheese, mixed dried herbs and red chilli flakes if desired.

It's a complete plate!

VALUE PER SERVING (1½ CUPS)	
Calories	314 kcal
Protein	9 gm
Fat	10 gm
Carbohydrates	45 gm
Fibre	2 gm
Calcium	196 mg
Iron	1 mg

Paneer Jalfrezi

Paneer and veggies combined in a pink gravy, to be served with rice or roti.

MAKES: 5 cups
SERVING SIZE: 1 cup

PREPARATION TIME: 10 mins
COOKING TIME: 25 mins

INGREDIENTS
125 gm paneer (see recipe on p. 237)
1 large onion, chopped into squares
5 medium tomatoes
¾ cup carrots, chopped moderately
½ cup French beans, chopped moderately
½ cup green peas, shelled
¾ cup cauliflower, separated into medium florets
¾ cup red and yellow bell peppers, chopped into squares
½ cup cold milk
½ tbsp cornflour
3 green chillies, chopped coarsely
½ tsp red chilli powder
2 tbsp tomato ketchup
1 tbsp sugar
¼ tsp black pepper powder
1 tbsp oil
Salt as per taste

METHOD

1. Drop the tomatoes in a pan of boiling water for 7–8 minutes. Drain and cool. Peel the blanched tomatoes, chop coarsely and grind in a mixer along with green chillies. Sieve the puree and keep aside.
2. Boil water in another pan. Add cauliflower and cook for 5–7 minutes. Drain and keep aside to cool.
3. Pressure-cook the French beans, carrots and peas. Cook for 1 whistle. Drain and keep aside.
4. Heat oil in a pan. Add onions; sauté until translucent.
5. Add the bell peppers; sauté for a minute.
6. Combine all the boiled vegetables, red chilli powder and salt, and sauté for 2 minutes.
7. Stir in the tomato puree, sugar, black pepper powder and salt. Simmer for 5 minutes.
8. In a separate bowl, dissolve cornflour in ½ cup cold milk. Add this to the vegetable mix. Simmer for another 2–3 minutes.
9. Dice the paneer into cubes and combine with the vegetable mix along with tomato ketchup.
10. Cook for another 2 minutes. Serve hot.

Complete your plate—with a bowl of steamed rice.

VALUE PER SERVING (1 CUP)			
Calories	195 kcal	Protein	7 gm
Fat	9 gm	Carbohydrates	17 gm
Fibre	2 gm	Calcium	318 mg
Iron	1 mg		

Rice Casserole

A flavourful rice and vegetable combination baked to perfection.

MAKES: 5 cups
SERVING SIZE: 1½ cups

PREPARATION TIME: 5 mins
COOKING TIME: 30 mins

INGREDIENTS
3 cups cold toned milk
½ cup rice, uncooked
1 medium onion, chopped coarsely
2 large tomatoes
¾ cup carrots, chopped finely
¾ cup French beans, chopped finely
½ cup peas, shelled
3 garlic cloves, chopped coarsely
50 gm cheese, grated
1 tsp red chilli flakes
3 tbsp cornflour
1 tsp powdered sugar
1 tbsp oil
Black pepper powder, as per taste
Salt as per taste

METHOD
1. Cook the rice in a pan of boiling water. Drain out the water and keep aside.

2. Boil the carrots, French beans and peas in 2–3 cups of water for 5–7 minutes. Drain and keep aside.

3. Drop the tomatoes in a pan of boiling water. Drain after 5 minutes and cool. Peel the blanched tomatoes and chop coarsely.

4. Put the blanched tomatoes, onion and garlic in a mixer and grind to a paste.

5. Heat the oil; sauté the onion–tomato paste for about 5 minutes.

6. Add the boiled vegetables and salt; sauté for about 2–3 minutes. Keep aside.

7. Preheat the oven at 160° C for 7–10 minutes. Grease a baking dish with a little butter.

8. Boil 2½ cups milk in a pan. Meanwhile, dissolve cornflour in the remaining ½ cup cold milk, and stir till dissolved completely. Add it to the boiling milk and stir constantly to prevent lumps from forming.

9. When it reaches a semi-thick consistency, add sugar. Remove from heat immediately and stir in the grated cheese to complete the white sauce.

10. Combine the cooked rice with the white sauce. Add red chilli flakes and salt. Keep aside.

11. In the greased baking dish, first spread the vegetables, then top them with the rice.

12. Bake for 10 minutes at 200° C. Add black pepper powder as per taste. Serve hot.

It's a complete plate!

VALUE PER SERVING (1½ CUPS)

Calories	341 kcal
Protein	14 gm
Fat	13 gm
Carbohydrates	28 gm
Fibre	2 gm
Calcium	442 mg
Iron	2 mg

Power-Packed Pav Bhaji

A healthy spin on the roadside favourite — so good you'll never know the difference!

MAKES: 8 cups
SERVING SIZE: 1 cup

PRE-PREPARATION TIME: 18–20 hrs
PREPARATION TIME: 10 mins
COOKING TIME: 45 mins

INGREDIENTS

1 cup green gram sprouts or ½ cup uncooked green gram
(Pre-prep: Soak for 6–8 hours, drain and keep covered for another 12 hours)
50 gm paneer (see recipe on p. 237), diced into tiny cubes
4 medium onions, chopped finely
4 medium tomatoes, chopped finely
2 medium capsicum, chopped finely
2 medium potatoes, boiled and peeled
¾ cup green peas, shelled
¾ cup cauliflower, chopped coarsely
¾ cup French beans, chopped finely
¾ cup carrots, chopped finely
12 large garlic cloves, peeled
5 tsp *pav bhaji masala*
Lemon juice, as per taste
4 tsp salt (or as per taste)
2 tbsp oil
2 tbsp fresh coriander leaves, chopped finely (for garnishing)
Butter or cheese (for garnishing)

METHOD

1. Pressure-cook the green gram sprouts and peas for 2 whistles; drain and reserve the stock.
2. Pressure-cook the French beans, carrots and cauliflower for 2 whistles; drain and reserve the stock.
3. In a mixer, grind the peeled garlic cloves with ¼ cup chopped tomatoes, red chilli powder, ⅓ cup water and a pinch of salt into a paste.
4. Heat the oil; sauté the onions until translucent.
5. Add capsicum; sauté for another 5 minutes.
6. Stir in the chilli–garlic paste; sauté for 10 minutes.
7. Add ½ cup stock and cook till the mixture leaves the sides of the pan.
8. Add the remaining tomatoes, *pav bhaji masala* and salt; sauté for 4–5 minutes. Keep adding stock as required.
9. Coarsely mash the boiled carrots, beans, cauliflower, peas, green gram sprouts and potatoes.
10. Combine all the mashed vegetables, the remaining stock and ½ cup water. Cook for 6–7 minutes. Add the paneer cubes and mix well. Remove from heat.
11. Add lemon juice just before serving. Garnish with a dollop of butter or cheese and coriander leaves.

Complete your plate—with *pav/chapatti* and a glass of buttermilk.

VALUE PER SERVING (1 CUP)			
Calories	140 kcal	Protein	5 gm
Fat	5 gm	Carbohydrates	17 gm
Fibre	2 gm	Calcium	113 mg
Iron	1 mg		

Spinach and Spaghetti Bake

A two-layered bake with added protein value of paneer.

MAKES: 8 cups
SERVING SIZE: 1½ cups

PREPARATION TIME: 10 mins
COOKING TIME: 30 mins

INGREDIENTS
1 cup fresh corn (from cob) or sweet corn kernels
100 gm spaghetti, uncooked
125 gm paneer (see recipe on p. 237)
3 cups spinach (300 gm leaves after cleaning)
2 green chillies, chopped finely
1 large onion, chopped finely
3 tsp dried mixed herbs (Italian seasoning)
1 tsp red chilli flakes
½ tsp butter
1 tbsp oil
4 cups toned milk
3 tbsp cornflour
2 tsp powdered sugar
Salt as per taste
Black pepper powder as per taste
20 gm cheese, grated (for garnishing)

METHOD
1. Clean the spinach thoroughly, discard the stems and chop coarsely.

2. Place the spinach in a pan. Cover and cook for 5–7 minutes (do not add water). Remove from heat and set aside to cool.

3. Meanwhile, pressure-cook the corn for 4–5 whistles. Drain and keep aside.

4. Boil water in a pan. Drop the spaghetti and boil for 10–12 minutes or till it is completely cooked.

5. Drain and wash the boiled spaghetti under running water. Spread on a flat surface and toss in ½ tsp oil to prevent it from sticking. Keep aside.

6. Squeeze out all the excess water from the cooled spinach and puree it in a mixer to form a thick, paste-like consistency.

7. Heat oil in a pan; sauté the green chillies for a minute.

8. Add onion; sauté till translucent.

9. Add the spinach puree and cook for about 4–5 minutes.

10. Cut the paneer into tiny cubes and add to the above.

11. Add salt as per taste and cook for another 2 minutes. Remove from heat and set aside. This is your spinach layer.

12. Preheat the oven at 160° C for 7–10 minutes.

13. To make the white sauce, boil 3 cups milk in a pan.

14. Meanwhile, dissolve cornflour in the remaining 1 cup cold milk, and stir till dissolved completely. Add it to the boiling milk and stir constantly to prevent lumps from forming.

15. When it reaches a semi-thick consistency, add ½ tsp black pepper powder, sugar and 1 tsp salt.

16. Add boiled corn and spaghetti to the white sauce.

17. Add mixed dried herbs and red chilli flakes; adjust the

taste by adding black pepper powder and salt as per taste.

18. Grease a baking dish with butter. Spread the spinach layer.
19. Top it with the spaghetti layer and garnish with grated cheese.
20. Bake for 8–10 minutes in the preheated oven and serve hot.

It's a complete plate!

VALUE PER SERVING (1½ CUPS)

Calories	315 kcal
Protein	16 gm
Fat	16 gm
Carbohydrates	26 gm
Fibre	1 gm
Calcium	292 mg
Iron	2 mg

Sweet and Sour Veg Chow Mein

A complete meal with noodles and veggies in a tangy tomato sauce.

MAKES: 10 cups
SERVING SIZE: 2 cups

PREPARATION TIME: 15 mins
COOKING TIME: 20 mins

INGREDIENTS

1 packet (150 gm) hakka noodles, uncooked
200 gm paneer (see recipe on p. 237), diced
1 medium tomato, chopped moderately
½ cup cabbage, julienned
½ cup onion, chopped into squares
½ cup yellow bell peppers, chopped into squares
½ cup French beans, sliced diagonally
½ cup greens of spring onion, chopped finely
½ cup carrots, sliced into thin semicircles
1 cup tomato puree
2-inch piece of ginger, julienned
8 large garlic cloves, chopped finely
1 tbsp cornflour
½ cup tomato ketchup
1 tbsp Schezwan sauce
4 tsp vinegar
2 tbsp soya sauce
1 tbsp oil
Salt as per taste

METHOD

1. Put the noodles in boiling water with a little salt and oil. Cook for 5–7 minutes or till done.
2. Drain and rinse in cold water. Coat with a little oil to prevent them from sticking and keep aside.
3. Heat oil in a pan. Sauté the ginger and garlic.
4. Add onions; sauté until translucent.
5. Add carrots; sauté for a minute.
6. Add bell peppers; sauté for a minute.
7. Add French beans; sauté for a minute.
8. Add cabbage; sauté for a minute.
9. Reduce heat and add tomato puree, ketchup, Schezwan sauce, soya sauce and vinegar. Cook for 2 minutes.
10. Add tomato and paneer cubes; mix well.
11. Add 2 cups water, greens of spring onions and salt. Cook for 2 more minutes.
12. Dissolve cornflour in 1 cup water and add to the above, stirring continuously.
13. Let it boil for 2–3 minutes till the sauce thickens.
14. Mix in the noodles, remove from heat and serve hot.

It's a complete plate!

VALUE PER SERVING (2 CUPS)

Calories	361 kcal	Protein	14 gm
Fat	14 gm	Carbohydrates	39 gm
Fibre	2 gm	Calcium	412 mg
Iron	1 mg		

Tangy Bean Curry with Green Leafy Paratha

The traditional kadhi with an added punch of proteins.

MAKES: 4 cups
SERVING SIZE: 1 cup

PRE-PREPARATION TIME: 6–8 hrs
PREPARATION TIME: 2 mins
COOKING TIME: 20 mins

INGREDIENTS

FOR CURRY
½ cup uncooked green gram **(Pre-prep: Soak for 6–8 hours or overnight)**
2 cups fresh curd
½ tsp cumin seeds
½ tsp red chilli powder
½ tsp turmeric powder
¼ tsp asafoetida (optional)
1 tsp ginger–green chilli paste
½ tsp mustard seeds
8–10 curry leaves
2 tbsp fresh coriander leaves, chopped finely
2 tsp sugar
2 tsp oil
Salt as per taste

FOR GREEN LEAFY PARATHA
2 cups wholewheat flour
1 cup fresh fenugreek leaves, chopped finely

1½ cups bottle gourd, grated
4 tbsp curd, sieved
½ tsp red chilli powder
½ tsp turmeric powder
1 tbsp oil (to add to the flour)
2 tbsp oil (for roasting the *parathas*)
Salt as per taste

METHOD FOR CURRY

1. Drain the soaked green gram and pressure-cook with 2 cups water for 1 whistle, and open immediately.
2. Heat oil in a pan. Add mustard seeds, cumin seeds, curry leaves and asafoetida.
3. When the cumin seeds change colour, add the ginger–green chilli paste.
4. Add turmeric powder and red chilli powder, and sauté for a minute.
5. Add the sieved curd and 1 cup water to the above.
6. Cook for 3 minutes, stirring continuously.
7. Add boiled green gram and salt. Cook for a few minutes and add the sugar.
8. Simmer for 5 minutes and add coriander leaves.
9. Remove from heat and serve hot with green leafy *paratha*.

Tip: Add salt only towards the end.

METHOD FOR GREEN LEAFY PARATHA

1. Sprinkle a little salt over the grated bottle gourd, keep aside for 5 minutes and then squeeze out all the liquid.

2. Combine with all the remaining ingredients (except oil) and knead into a soft dough. Do not add water.
3. Rest the dough for at least 15 minutes, keeping it covered with a muslin cloth.
4. Divide the dough into twelve equal portions and roll out a 5-inch *paratha* with each portion.
5. Roast the *paratha* on a *tava* using ½ tsp oil, flipping it over to ensure both sides are evenly golden brown. Serve hot with the curry.

VALUE PER SERVING (1 CUP CURRY)

Calories	126 kcal
Protein	6 gm
Fat	5 gm
Carbohydrates	14 gm
Fibre	0.5 gm
Calcium	141 mg
Iron	1 mg

VALUE PER SERVING (2 PARATHAS)

Calories	156 kcal
Protein	5 gm
Fat	7 gm
Carbohydrates	25 gm
Fibre	1 gm
Calcium	178 mg
Iron	2 mg

Vegetable Frankie

A crunchy and tangy vegetable frankie.

MAKES: 6
SERVING SIZE: 2

PREPARATION TIME: 10 mins
COOKING TIME: 20 mins

INGREDIENTS
½ cup wholewheat flour
½ cup all-purpose flour
2 large potatoes, boiled, peeled and mashed
1 large onion, sliced thinly
1 cup cabbage, shredded
¾ cup carrots, julienned
1 medium capsicum, julienned
3 tbsp fresh coriander leaves, chopped finely
¼ tsp turmeric powder
½ tsp *chaat* masala
½ tsp powdered sugar
Juice of ½ lemon
2 tbsp hot and sweet tomato ketchup
1 tbsp vinegar
2 tbsp oil
Salt as per taste

METHOD
1. Combine wholewheat flour, all-purpose flour, salt and
    ½ tsp oil.

2. Knead into a soft dough using warm water. Rest the dough for about 20 minutes.
3. Divide the dough into six equal parts.
4. Roll out the portions into round rotis around 5 inches in diameter.
5. Heat a *tava* and semi-roast the rotis on both sides without using any oil. Keep aside.
6. Heat oil in a pan. Add onions and sauté till translucent.
7. Add mashed potatoes, turmeric powder, powdered sugar, *chaat* masala and salt. Mix well.
8. Turn off the flame and add coriander leaves and lemon juice. Divide the potato mix into six equal portions.
9. To make the frankie, take one roti and spread ¼ tsp vinegar on it.
10. Then spread 1 tsp hot and sweet tomato ketchup.
11. Spread one portion of the potato filling in the centre of each roti. Garnish with cabbage, carrot, capsicum.
12. Now roll up tightly to make the frankie and roast on a *tava* using oil until brown spots start appearing.
13. With a pizza cutter, cut each frankie diagonally from the centre and serve hot!

Complete the plate—with a glass of buttermilk.

VALUE PER SERVING (2 FRANKIES)

Calories	347 kcal	Protein	7 gm
Fat	9 gm	Carbohydrates	59 gm
Fibre	2 gm	Calcium	117 mg
Iron	3 mg		

Party Foods

Introduction

Birthday parties and day-spends call for especially scrummy food. The good news is that you can now be the favourite mommy on the block as well as avoid feeding the children junk and unwholesome foods. Children tend to binge on their favourite junk food during parties. In the recipes that follow, party foods have been perfected to contain the right balance of nutrients. They are not junk as they have low calorie content, but could fool you as they are super yummy! Snacks like Mini Hummus Rolls, Nachos Bhel and Mini Sliders are not only stomach-filling and a big hit with children, they also take care of their health and nutrition intake. The coolers are a good and tasty replacement for aerated drinks.

Mini Sliders

Mini burgers stuffed with paneer, mushrooms and zucchini patties.

MAKES: 16
SERVING SIZE: 2

PREPARATION TIME: 10 mins
COOKING TIME: 20 mins

INGREDIENTS
16 mini burger buns
2 cups spinach (100 gm after cleaning)
½ cup mushrooms, chopped finely
½ medium zucchini, peeled and grated finely
125 gm paneer (see recipe on p. 237), diced into tiny cubes
1½ slices white bread (for breadcrumbs)
2 green chillies, chopped finely
3 garlic cloves, chopped finely
1-inch piece of ginger, grated finely
¼ tsp black pepper powder
1 tsp dry mango powder
½ tsp red chilli powder
½ tsp *garam masala*
2 tbsp oil
Pinch of sugar
Salt as per taste

FOR SERVING:

16 lettuce leaves (torn roughly in circles to the size of the burger bun)

16 small slices of onion

16 small slices of tomato

½ cup curd dip (see recipe on p. 236) or mayonnaise

METHOD

1. Preheat the oven at 160° C for 7–10 minutes.
2. Put the spinach in a broad pan with ½ cup water. Add a pinch of sugar and salt. Cover and cook for about 5 minutes or till the spinach wilts completely. Drain and cool.
3. Sprinkle salt on the grated zucchini and keep aside.
4. To make breadcrumbs, toast the bread in a pop-up toaster until brown. Cool and grind to a fine powder in a mixer.
5. Heat 1 tbsp oil in a pan. Add garlic, ginger and green chillies; sauté for half a minute.
6. Add mushrooms; sauté for one minute.
7. Add the diced paneer; sauté for another minute.
8. Squeeze out all the excess water from the zucchini and add it to the above; sauté for a minute.
9. Season with red chilli powder, *garam masala*, dry mango powder, black pepper powder and salt; sauté for 2 minutes.
10. Squeeze out all the excess water from the spinach and chop roughly.
11. Add the spinach to the above mix and cook for 1 minute. Set aside to cool.

12. When cooled, give this veggie mix a quick whisk in a mixer.
13. Transfer to a bowl, add the bread crumbs and mix well.
14. Refrigerate the mix for about 30 minutes.
15. Divide the mix into sixteen equal portions.
16. Dust some flour on your hands and make small patties of each portion.
17. Heat a heavy-bottom pan and roast the patties with 1 tbsp oil till golden brown on each side.
18. Apply a little butter on the top and bottom portion of the burger buns and warm them in the preheated oven.
19. Slice the warm burger bun into half.
20. Place a lettuce leaf on the lower half of the burger and put one patty over it.
21. Top with ½ tbsp of the curd dip or mayonnaise (optional)
22. Then top with slices of onions and tomato.
23. Cover with the upper half of the burger.
24. Secure with a toothpick and serve with ketchup.

VALUE PER SERVING (2 MINI SLIDERS)	
Calories	230 kcal
Protein	10 gm
Fat	8 gm
Carbohydrates	30 gm
Fibre	3 gm
Calcium	224 mg
Iron	1 mg

Creamy Corn Crackers/ Pancakes

Crispy crackers topped with creamy corn and spinach.

MAKES: 12
SERVING SIZE: 2

PREPARATION TIME: 10 mins
COOKING TIME: 15 mins

INGREDIENTS
12 cream cracker biscuits
3 cups spinach (180 gm after cleaning)
1¼ cup fresh corn (from cob) or sweet corn kernels
1 large onion, chopped finely
3 tsp garlic, grated
1½ tsp ginger–green chilli paste
100 gm cheese, grated
1½ tbsp cornflour
¼ tsp black pepper powder
1 tbsp butter
Pinch of sugar
Salt as per taste

METHOD
1. Pressure-cook the sweet corn kernels with 3 cups water and ½ tsp salt for 5 whistles. Drain and keep aside.
2. If using fresh corn off the cob, cook it in boiling water with ½ tsp salt for 3–4 minutes. Drain and keep aside.

3. Heat a broad non-stick pan and place the spinach in it with ¾ cup water. Add a pinch of salt and sugar. Cover and cook for 5 minutes or till it wilts. Drain and cool. Chop coarsely and keep aside.
4. Heat butter in a pan. Sauté the garlic and ginger–green chilli paste.
5. Add onions; sauté till translucent.
6. Combine boiled corn; sauté for 2 minutes. Add black pepper powder and salt as per taste.
7. Add the chopped spinach; sauté for another minute.
8. Dissolve the cornflour in ⅓ cup water. Add to the above mix. Stir continuously till it coats the spinach mix completely.
9. Turn off the flame and add 3½ tbsp grated cheese. Keep aside.
10. Top each cream cracker biscuit with 2 tbsp of the corn and spinach mix. Garnish with some grated cheese. Cut into triangles and serve immediately.

NOTE: The photograph for this dish has been shot with the filling on a pancake, but to make it quicker and easier, cream crackers have been used in the recipe.

VALUE PER SERVING (2 CRACKERS)

Calories	152 kcal	Protein	5 gm
Fat	11 gm	Carbohydrates	8 gm
Calcium	134 mg	Fibre	1 gm
Iron	1.5 mg		

Nachos Bhel

Kids' favourite nachos made nutritious with a mix of kidney beans and corn.

MAKES: 7 cups
SERVING SIZE: 1 cup

PRE-PREPARATION TIME: 6–8 hrs
PREPARATION TIME: 20 mins
COOKING TIME: 20 mins

INGREDIENTS

FOR BHEL

½ cup uncooked kidney beans **(Pre-prep: Soak for 6–8 hours)**
1 cup fresh corn (from cob) or sweet corn kernels
1 cup red bell peppers, chopped moderately
1 cup capsicum, chopped moderately
2 medium onions, chopped moderately
150 gm paneer (see recipe on p. 237), diced into tiny cubes
2 green chillies, chopped finely
½ tsp black pepper powder
85 gm tortilla chips
2 tbsp butter
Salt as per taste

FOR SOUR CREAM

2 tbsp garlic mayonnaise
2 tbsp fresh cream
4 tbsp fresh curd

METHOD

FOR SOUR CREAM:

Combine all the ingredients for the sour cream, mix well and refrigerate.

FOR BHEL:

1. Pressure-cook the kidney beans with 3 cups water and ½ tsp salt for 4–5 whistles. Drain and keep aside.
2. Pressure-cook the corn for 4 whistles. Drain and keep aside.
3. Heat butter in a pan. Add green chillies and onions; sauté till the onions are translucent.
4. Add bell peppers and capsicum. Sauté for 2 minutes.
5. Add boiled corn. Sauté for 2 minutes.
6. Add boiled kidney beans, black pepper powder and salt. Cook for 2 minutes.
7. Add paneer and cook for another minute. Season with oregano and chilli flakes if using unflavoured paneer.

TO SERVE:

1. Put 1 cup of the kidney beans mixture in a serving bowl.
2. Crush about 3 triangles of tortilla chips on it.
3. Drizzle 1 tbsp salsa sauce over it (see recipe on p. 239).
4. Top with 1 tbsp sour cream and serve fresh!

VARIATION: You can alternatively use flavoured paneer (see recipe on p. 237) or feta cheese.

VALUE PER SERVING (1 CUP)

Calories	264 kcal	Protein	9 gm
Fat	14 gm	Carbohydrates	5 gm
Fibre	2 gm	Calcium	95 mg
Iron	1 mg		

Orange Twister

Kids' favourite fruits blended together to make a tangy sip.

MAKES: 2 glasses
SERVING SIZE: 1 glass

INGREDIENTS
1 medium pear, peeled and chopped
2 medium oranges, peeled, segmented, seeds and white thread removed (leave white pithy part)
1 tbsp sugar
1 cup water
2 ice cubes

METHOD
1. Combine all the ingredients and blend together in a mixer.
2. Strain and serve chilled in a tall glass.

VALUE PER SERVING (1 GLASS)

Calories	105 kcal
Protein	0.5 gm
Fat	0.3 gm
Carbohydrates	25 gm
Fibre	1 gm
Calcium	26 mg
Iron	0.5 mg

Beany Green Quesadillas

Nutritious green quesadillas with a cheesy filling of vegetables.

MAKES: 7
SERVING SIZE: 1

PREPARATION TIME: 10 mins
COOKING TIME: 30 mins

INGREDIENTS
1 cup wholewheat flour
¾ cup all-purpose flour
2 cups spinach (100 gm after cleaning)
1 cup mushrooms, chopped finely
½ cup fresh corn (from cob) or sweet corn kernels
¾ cup canned baked beans
⅓ cup yellow bell peppers, chopped finely
2 bulbs of spring onions, chopped finely
½ cup greens of spring onion, chopped finely
100 gm cheese, grated
¼ cup cold milk
1 tbsp cornflour
2½ tbsp butter
1 tsp oil
½ tsp sugar
½ tsp black pepper powder
Salt as per taste

METHOD

1. Place the spinach in a pan along with ½ cup water and a pinch of salt and sugar. Cover and let it cook for 5 minutes or till it wilts. Drain and cool.
2. Squeeze half of the water from the cooled spinach and then put the spinach in a mixer; whisk to a puree.
3. Combine the wholewheat flour, all-purpose flour, spinach puree, 1 tsp oil and salt as per taste. Knead it into a dough and let it rest for a while.
4. Meanwhile, pressure-cook the corn with 3 cups of water and ½ tsp salt for 5 whistles. Strain and keep aside. (Omit this step if using fresh corn off the cob.)
5. Once cooled, give the corn a quick whisk in the mixer, so that the kernels are crushed but not pureed.
6. Strain and lightly mash the baked beans. Keep aside.
7. Heat 1 tbsp butter and sauté the onions. Add bell peppers and salt as per taste; sauté for a minute.
8. Add corn; sauté for 3 minutes.
9. Add the mushrooms and the greens of spring onions; sauté for 2–3 minutes.
10. Add the mashed beans, black pepper powder and salt as per taste; sauté for another minute.
11. Dissolve the cornflour in cold milk and add to the above mix.
12. Cook for 2 minutes till the mix is semi-dry. Remove from heat.
13. Add 2 tbsp grated cheese and combine well. Keep aside.
14. Divide the dough into fourteen equal portions and roll out thin rotis with each portion.
15. Partially roast all the rotis on a *tava* and keep aside.

TO SERVE:

16. Spread ¼ cup of the bean and vegetable mix on one roti.
17. Garnish with 1 tbsp grated cheese.
18. Cover with another roti and press down firmly.
19. Using a small amount of butter, roast on a heated *tava* until brown spots appear on the surface. Flip over and repeat for the other side.
20. Cut into four slices with a pizza cutter and serve with curd dip (see recipe on p. 236).

VALUE PER SERVING (1 QUESADILLA)

Calories	269 kcal
Protein	10 gm
Fat	12 gm
Carbohydrates	29 gm
Fibre	1 gm
Calcium	210 mg
Iron	2 mg

Tomato and Paneer Bruschetta

All-time favourite bruschettas unjunked by adding protein punch of paneer.

MAKES: 14
SERVING SIZE: 2

PREPARATION TIME: 5 mins
COOKING TIME: 25 mins

INGREDIENTS

½ French baguette (narrow French stick loaf) (150 gm), cut into 14 oval slices
125 gm paneer (see recipe on p. 237)
3 medium tomatoes (ripe and firm)
⅓ cup yellow bell peppers, chopped finely
3 tbsp stalk and greens of spring onion, chopped finely
2 tbsp fresh basil leaves, chopped finely
7 garlic cloves, grated
75 gm cheese, grated
1 tsp red chilli flakes
1½ tsp dried oregano
¼ tsp black pepper powder
Salt as per taste
2 tbsp melted butter
1 tbsp olive oil

METHOD

1. Preheat the oven at 160° C for 7–10 minutes.
2. Cut the paneer into small cubes.

3. To prepare the garlic butter mix, combine the grated garlic, melted butter, chilli flakes, oregano and salt. Keep aside.
4. Cut each tomato into 4 parts. Core and discard the pulp and the seeds. Then moderately chop the remaining portion.
5. Heat the olive oil. Add bell peppers and sauté for 30 seconds.
6. Add the greens and stalks of spring onion; sauté for 30 seconds.
7. Add tomatoes and basil leaves; sauté for a minute.
8. Season with black pepper powder and salt.
9. Remove from flame and combine the paneer cubes.
10. Toast the baguette slices lightly in preheated oven.
11. Then apply the garlic butter on each slice. Top it with the paneer and tomato mix (approximately 1½ heaped tbsp)
12. Garnish with ½ tsp grated cheese on each slice.
13. Bake in the preheated oven for 5 minutes. Serve hot.

VALUE PER SERVING (2 BRUSCHETTAS)

Calories	232 kcal
Protein	9 gm
Fat	12 gm
Carbohydrates	18 gm
Fibre	1 gm
Calcium	268 mg
Iron	1 mg

Mini Hummus Rolls

Hummus smeared on bread slices, filled with crunchy vegetable mix and shaped into mini rolls.

MAKES: 12
SERVING SIZE: 2

PRE-PREPARATION TIME: 6–8 hrs
PREPARATION TIME: 5 mins
COOKING TIME: 20 mins

INGREDIENTS

12 slices white bread
¼ cup fresh curd
½ cup uncooked chickpeas **(Pre-prep: Soak for 6–8 hours or overnight)**
1½ cups carrots, grated finely
1½ cups cabbage, shredded finely
1 cup zucchini, unpeeled, grated finely
¼ cup red bell peppers, chopped finely
4 large garlic cloves, chopped coarsely
2 green chillies, chopped coarsely
1½ tbsp vinegar
1 tbsp butter
1 tbsp oil
Salt as per taste

METHOD

1. Pressure-cook the chickpeas in 3 cups water and ½ tsp salt for 7–8 whistles. Drain and cool.

2. Sauté the bell peppers with ¼ tsp salt and oil, till soft. Keep aside to cool.
3. Put the chickpeas, bell peppers, curd, garlic, green chillies, vinegar and 1½ tsp salt in a mixer. Grind to a thick paste. Keep aside.
4. Heat oil in a pan; sauté carrots and zucchini for a minute.
5. Add cabbage and salt; sauté for 2 minutes. Remove from heat and keep aside.
6. Slice off and discard the crust of each slice of bread. Using a rolling pin, flatten each slice as much as possible.
7. With a butter knife, spread 1½ tbsp of the chickpea paste on each flattened slice.
8. Evenly spread 1½ tbsp of the vegetable mix over it.
9. Tightly roll up each slice and apply a small amount of butter on the exposed sides of the roll.
10. Roast each roll on a non-stick *tava*, flipping it over from time to time, until evenly golden brown on both sides.
11. To serve, cut each roll into 3 pieces using a pizza cutter. Serve with green chutney and/or ketchup.

VALUE PER SERVING (2 ROLLS)

Calories	227 kcal	Protein	7 gm
Fat	7 gm	Carbohydrates	33 gm
Fibre	1 gm	Calcium	18 mg
Iron	1 mg		

Vegetable Sweet Corn Soup

A quick Chinese appetiser.

MAKES: 7½ cups
SERVING SIZE: 1½ cups

PREPARATION TIME: 15 mins
COOKING TIME: 20 mins

INGREDIENTS
2 cups sweet corn kernels
½ cup French beans, chopped finely
½ cup carrots, chopped finely
¼ cup bulbs of spring onion, chopped finely
¼ cup stalks of spring onion, chopped finely
¼ cup greens of spring onion, chopped finely
1-inch piece of ginger, grated
2 tbsp cornflour
2 tsp soya sauce
1 tbsp vinegar
2 tbsp hot and sweet tomato ketchup
2 tbsp fresh cream
¼ tsp black pepper powder
1 tbsp butter
Salt as per taste

METHOD
1. Pressure-cook the sweet corn kernels for 6–7 whistles. Drain and retain the stock. Set both aside.
2. Boil water in a pan. Cook the carrots and French beans

in it for 7–8 minutes. Drain, retain the stock and set aside.

3. Blend half the quantity of the boiled corn in a mixer with a little water (three quick churns).

4. Heat butter in a pan. Add the ginger and bulbs of spring onions; sauté for a minute.

5. Add the carrots, French beans and stalks of spring onions; sauté for a minute.

6. Combine the blended corn and 1 cup of the retained corn stock.

7. Dissolve the cornflour in 3 tbsp water and add to the above.

8. Add the remaining boiled corn, 1 cup of the corn stock and 2 cups of the reserved vegetable stock.

9. Add 1½ cups water. Season with black pepper powder and salt.

10. Add greens of spring onions and cream; cook for another minute.

11. Add the ketchup, soya sauce and vinegar.

12. Cook for few more minutes. Serve hot.

VALUE PER SERVING (1½ CUPS)

Calories	116 kcal
Protein	3 gm
Fat	3 gm
Carbohydrates	18 gm
Fibre	1 gm
Calcium	30 mg
Iron	1 mg

Pasta in Pink Sauce

Colourful pasta cooked in kids' favourite combination of red and white sauce.

MAKES: 7½ cups
SERVING SIZE: 1½ cups

PREPARATION TIME: 5 mins
COOKING TIME: 30 mins

INGREDIENTS
2 cups pasta (macaroni, farfalle or fusilli), uncooked
1 cup canned baked beans
4 baby corns, slit lengthwise and parboiled
⅓ cup red bell peppers, julienned
⅓ cup yellow bell peppers, julienned
4 medium tomatoes
1 medium onion, sliced thinly
¼ cup celery stalks, sliced thinly
2 tbsp fresh basil leaves, chopped finely
3–4 garlic cloves, chopped finely
2 tbsp hot and sweet tomato ketchup
1½ tbsp cornflour
1½ cups toned milk
1 tbsp olive oil
1 tsp sugar
½ tsp black pepper powder
Salt as per taste
3 tbsp cheese, grated (for garnishing)

METHOD

1. Preheat the oven at 160° C for 7–10 minutes. Grease a baking dish with a little butter. Keep aside.
2. Drop the tomatoes in a pan of boiling water. Drain after 5 minutes and cool. Peel the blanched tomatoes and chop coarsely. Grind in a mixer and sieve the puree.
3. Boil the pasta in plenty of salted water till it is al dente. Drain and set aside.
4. Heat olive oil in a pan. Sauté garlic until fragrant.
5. Add onions; sauté until translucent.
6. Add bell peppers and celery stalks; sauté for 1 minute.
7. Add baby corn; sauté for ½ minute. Season with black pepper powder and salt.
8. Add basil leaves and tomato puree. Cook for 2 minutes.
9. Add baked beans, tomato ketchup and sugar. Cook for 1 minute.
10. Meanwhile, stir the cornflour in the milk. Mix until it dissolves completely.
11. Add it to the beans mix. Cook for 3–4 minutes, stirring continuously as the sauce thickens. Adjust salt as per taste. Keep aside.
12. Refresh the pasta by placing it in a sieve and running it under cold water. Add the pasta to the pink sauce.
13. Spread the pasta in a greased baking dish. Garnish with grated cheese.
14. Bake in preheated oven for about 8–10 minutes. Serve hot.

VALUE PER SERVING (1½ CUPS)

Calories	235 kcal
Protein	10 gm
Fat	7 gm
Carbohydrates	33 gm
Fibre	1 gm
Calcium	202 mg
Iron	2 mg

Minty Fruity Cooler

A cool thirst quencher flavoured with mint for that quick sip after an outdoor play.

MAKES: 1 glass
SERVING SIZE: 1 glass

INGREDIENTS
½ cup grapes, rinsed
¼ cup pineapple, chopped coarsely
¼ cup fresh mint leaves (a few extra leaves to garnish)
1 tsp lemon juice
1 tsp powdered sugar
½ cup club soda
1 tsp chia seeds/*falooda* seeds, soaked (optional)

METHOD
1. Crush the mint leaves and squeeze out the juice. Retain the juice and discard the leaves.
2. Combine the grapes and pineapple and blend in a mixer.
3. Strain and add the mint juice.
4. Add sugar, lime juice, soda and chia seeds.
5. Garnish with a few sprigs of mint leaves.
6. Add a little crushed ice and serve chilled in a tall glass.

VALUE PER SERVING (1 GLASS)

Calories	88 kcal
Protein	0.5 gm
Fat	0.3 gm
Carbohydrates	21 gm
Fibre	2 gm
Calcium	20 mg
Iron	1 mg

Desserts

Introduction

You must think I am crazy for recommending desserts in a book on nutrition and health! But don't worry, because these low-calorie, delicious desserts are great for children. These recipes contain the goodness of milk, power of nuts and vital fruits. I hear parents complaining that kids these days are addicted to Western desserts like cakes, pastries, doughnuts, etc. But why blame the West? Our Indian *mithai*s are equally high in calories. In the following recipes, therefore, you will find a delectable and healthy infusion of Indian and Western tastes which a child can relish. Believe me, your child will ask for more!

Apple and Vermicelli Kheer

Traditional Indian kheer made with vermicelli and apple.

MAKES: 6 cups
SERVING SIZE: ¾ cup

PREPARATION TIME: 5 mins
COOKING TIME: 30 mins (plus refrigeration)

INGREDIENTS
1 cup vermicelli, uncooked
1 large apple
1½ litres toned milk
6 tbsp sugar
¼ tsp cinnamon powder
1 tsp *ghee*

METHOD
1. Heat the milk in a pan. Continue boiling till it reduces to almost half (or about 800 ml). Keep stirring the milk intermittently to prevent it from sticking to the bottom of the pan.
2. Meanwhile, heat *ghee* in a non-stick saucepan. Roast the vermicelli till it turns golden brown (this takes about 4–5 minutes).
3. Once the milk has reduced to half, add the roasted vermicelli and cook for about 5 minutes.
4. Then add sugar and cook for another 5 minutes, stirring continuously.
5. Add cinnamon powder and mix well.

6. Remove from heat, cool and then refrigerate.
7. Just before serving the *kheer*, peel and cut the apple into small cubes and add it to the chilled *kheer*.
8. Serve chilled.

TIP: You can always stew the cubed apple and then add it to the *kheer*.

SHELF LIFE: Keep refrigerated and consume within 24 hours.

VALUE PER SERVING (¾ CUP)

Calories	199 kcal
Protein	7 gm
Fat	6 gm
Carbohydrates	28 gm
Fibre	0 gm
Calcium	284 mg
Iron	0 mg

Brownies with Cream Cheese

Kids' all-time favourite walnut brownies enhanced with the nutrition of brown rice.

MAKES: 25
SERVING SIZE: 2

PREPARATION TIME: 10 mins
COOKING TIME: 40 mins (plus baking time)

INGREDIENTS
⅓ cup brown rice, uncooked
¾ cup walnuts, chopped finely
2 eggs
4 tbsp cream cheese
½ cup self-raising flour
1 cup powdered sugar
1 tsp baking soda
1 tsp baking powder
4 tbsp cocoa powder
4 tbsp icing sugar
½ tsp vanilla essence
5 tbsp butter

METHOD
1. Preheat the oven at 180° C for 7–10 minutes.
2. Pressure-cook the brown rice with 2 cups water for 8 whistles. The rice should be slightly overcooked. Strain and keep aside. Let it cool.
3. Melt the butter in a pan and remove from the flame.

4. Pour the melted butter into a large mixing bowl; add the sugar and eggs. Whisk thoroughly.
5. Add cocoa, flour and vanilla essence. Whisk the batter again.
6. Blend the brown rice in a mixer to form a smooth paste.
7. Add the blended rice to the batter; whisk for at least 5–6 minutes to form a smooth batter.
8. Add ½ cup walnuts, baking powder and baking soda.
9. Whisk once again for 4–5 minutes.
10. Grease the bottom and sides of a square cake tin of 7" x 7" with a little butter.
11. Dust some cocoa powder on the greased area. Upturn the tin, tap and shake off the excess cocoa.
12. Pour the brownie batter in the tin.
13. Bake in the preheated oven for 30–35 minutes. Keep aside to cool.
14. Meanwhile, to make the icing, sift the icing sugar in a bowl. Combine well with the cream cheese.
15. Upturn the tin and remove the brownie cake on a chopping board.
16. Turn over the brownie cake gently and spread the icing evenly over the top.
17. Garnish with the remaining chopped walnuts.
18. Cut vertically and then horizontally to make about 25 equal blocks.
19. Serve warm.

VALUE PER SERVING (2 BROWNIES)

Calories	169 kcal
Protein	3 gm
Fat	9 gm
Carbohydrates	18 gm
Fibre	1 gm
Calcium	16 mg
Iron	0 mg

Date and Walnut Pops

A super quick dessert with orange biscuits which even children can make themselves.

MAKES: 10
SERVING SIZE: 2

PREPARATION TIME: 2 mins
COOKING TIME: 10 mins (plus refrigeration)

INGREDIENTS
⅓ cup dates, deseeded
6 whole walnuts, chopped finely
4 double-decker wafer biscuits, orange-flavoured (Pickwick wafer biscuits)
3 tbsp desiccated coconut (fresh and pure white in colour)
1 tbsp orange juice (Tropicana)
2 tbsp chocolate powder

METHOD
1. Cut the dates into thin, long strips. Then chop finely. Lightly mash with hands.
2. Crush the biscuits finely.
3. In a large mixing bowl, combine the dates, walnuts and biscuits.
4. Add 1 tbsp desiccated coconut and orange juice.
5. Mix well to form into dough and divide into twelve equal portions.
6. Shape each portion into a small ball. Keep aside.

7. Put the chocolate powder and the remaining desiccated coconut in two separate plates.
8. Roll each ball first in the chocolate powder and then in the desiccated coconut.
9. Serve immediately, or chill for an hour in the refrigerator and serve.

TIPS:
1. Make sure that the desiccated coconut is fresh and white in colour; refrigerate it to maintain its freshness and colour.
2. Insert small straws for making date and walnut pops.

SHELF LIFE: Keep refrigerated and consume within four days.

VALUE PER SERVING (2 POPS)

Calories	84 kcal
Protein	1 gm
Fat	4 gm
Carbohydrates	11 gm
Fibre	1 gm
Calcium	15 mg
Iron	1 mg

Flavoured Yoghurt Shots

A quick and simple substitute for ice cream.

MAKES: 6
SERVING SIZE: 1 shot glass

PREPARATION TIME: 2 mins
COOKING TIME: 5 mins (plus refrigeration)

INGREDIENTS
250 gm yoghurt (strawberry-flavoured or plain)
½ cup sweetened condensed milk
6 tsp oranges, segmented and chopped
6 tsp red grapes, chopped
2 tbsp strawberry crush (or any other flavour)

METHOD
1. If using plain yoghurt, whisk the yoghurt and strawberry crush. You can also use pineapple, mint or any other flavour of your choice.
2. If using flavoured yoghurt, omit step 1.
3. In a large mixing bowl, combine the yoghurt and condensed milk.
4. Whisk thoroughly to form a smooth mix.
5. Pour the mix in equal measures in six shot glasses.
6. Refrigerate for 3–4 hours till it sets in a jelly-like consistency.
7. Just before serving, garnish each shot glass with 1 tsp each of chopped orange and grapes (or any other fruits of your choice).
8. Serve chilled.

SHELF LIFE: Keep refrigerated and consume within 48 hours.

VALUE PER SERVING (1 SHOT GLASS)

Calories	108 kcal
Protein	3 gm
Fat	2 gm
Carbohydrates	19 gm
Fibre	0 gm
Calcium	48 mg
Iron	0 mg

Fruity Praline Cream

Thick, sweetened yoghurt blended with crispy bits of fruit and crunchy praline.

MAKES: 3
SERVING SIZE: ½ cup

PRE-PREPARATION TIME: 3 hrs
PREPARATION TIME: 2 mins
COOKING TIME: 10 mins (plus refrigeration)

INGREDIENTS
½ medium apple (or any other fruit of your choice)
½ medium pear
5 cups fresh curd **(Pre-prep: Hang in a muslin cloth for 3 hours)**
8 almonds, chopped coarsely
6 tbsp granulated sugar
6 tbsp powdered sugar
½ tsp cinnamon powder
¼ tsp *ghee*

METHOD
1. Grease a plate with *ghee* and keep aside.
2. To make praline, heat the granulated sugar in a pan, stirring continuously with a fork, until it melts and is caramelized to a golden brown liquid.
3. Remove from heat and immediately add almonds.
4. Quickly spread the praline mixture on the greased plate.

5. Once the mixture has set and cooled completely, break it with your hands and churn it in a mixer for just 2 seconds. This is your praline. Set it aside.
6. Strain the hung curd through a muslin cloth. Stir in cinnamon and powdered sugar.
7. Peel the apple and pear; cut into tiny cubes and immediately add to the sweetened curd to prevent the fruits from browning.
8. Mix in three fourths of the praline. Refrigerate.
9. To serve, pour the fruit cream into six small cups and garnish each with the remaining praline. Serve chilled.

SHELF LIFE: Keep refrigerated and consume within 48 hours.

VALUE PER SERVING (½ CUP)

Calories	217 kcal
Protein	5 gm
Fat	7 gm
Carbohydrates	33 gm
Fibre	0 gm
Calcium	252 mg
Iron	0.5 mg

Jello on Banoffee

A spin-off from the classic Banoffee pie topped with jello cubes.

MAKES: 4½ cups
SERVING SIZE: ¾ cup

PRE-PREPARATION TIME: 2 hrs
PREPARATION TIME: 5 mins
COOKING TIME: 10 mins (plus refrigeration)

INGREDIENTS
8 Marie biscuits
1½ large bananas
4 tbsp condensed milk
2 tbsp powdered sugar
2 cups toned milk
1½ tbsp custard powder, vanilla flavour
½ packet jelly
½ tsp vanilla essence

METHOD
1. Make the jelly as per the method given on the packet.
2. Set the jelly liquid in a flat bottom shallow dish (to cut into cubes later). Refrigerate for 2 hours.
3. Heat 1 cup milk in a pan. Meanwhile, dissolve the custard powder in the remaining milk.
4. Add the custard mixture to the boiling milk. Continue to cook over low heat, stirring constantly, until the milk thickens.
5. Add sugar and vanilla essence and keep aside to cool.

6. Take a baking dish approximately 7" x 7" in size. Crush all the biscuits into the baking dish.
7. Pour 4 tbsp condensed milk over the crushed biscuits.
8. Peel and chop the bananas into ¼-inch-thick slices. Lay out the banana slices evenly over the condensed milk.
9. Pour the custard evenly all over the banana layer.
10. Dice the jelly into cubes. Top the custard with jelly cubes.
11. Refrigerate for 2 hours. Serve chilled.

VARIATION: This recipe can be made in individual bowls by crushing two biscuits in each bowl.

SHELF LIFE: Keep refrigerated and consume within 48 hours.

VALUE PER SERVING (¾ CUP)

Calories	174 kcal
Protein	4 gm
Fat	3 gm
Carbohydrates	32 gm
Fibre	0 gm
Calcium	104 mg
Iron	0 mg

Mango Chenna Payesh

Classic Bengali dessert, paneer kheer with an added twist of fruit.

MAKES: 5
SERVING SIZE: ½ cup

PREPARATION TIME: 5 mins
COOKING TIME: 30 mins (plus refrigeration)

INGREDIENTS
8 cups toned milk
6 tbsp sugar
Juice of 1 lemon
2 medium, ripe alphonso mangoes (or any other seasonal fresh fruit)

METHOD
1. Pour 5 cups (1000 ml) milk in a pan.
2. Boil the milk until it reduces to a little less than half (400 ml) and stir intermittently to make sure that the milk does not stick to the pan.
3. When the milk in the first pan reduces to around 400 ml, add sugar and continue heating on slow flame for 3–4 minutes.
4. Meanwhile, in a second pan, heat the remaining milk.
5. When the milk in the second pan comes to a boil, turn off the flame and immediately add lemon juice, stirring until the milk curdles. Strain completely. This is the *chenna*. Crumble the *chenna* with your hands and keep aside.

6. Stir in the crumbled *chenna* into the milk and mix well. Remove from heat and stir well. Keep aside to cool. This is the *chenna payesh*.
7. Peel and chop the mangoes into tiny cubes.
8. When the *chenna payesh* cools completely, combine the mangoes.
9. Refrigerate and serve chilled.

VARIATION: Instead of mangoes, you can add the fruit of your choice (preferably pomegranate, strawberry, grapes).

SHELF LIFE: Keep refrigerated and consume within 24 hours.

VALUE PER SERVING (½ CUP)

Calories	145 kcal
Protein	5 gm
Fat	4 gm
Carbohydrates	20 gm
Fibre	0 gm
Calcium	243 mg
Iron	0 mg

Quick Pineapple Soufflé

Pineapple soufflé made the quick and easy way.

MAKES: 7 cups
SERVING SIZE: ¾ cup

PREPARATION TIME: 5 mins
COOKING TIME: 30 mins (plus refrigeration)

INGREDIENTS
9 pineapple slices, canned
1½ cups canned pineapple syrup
1 packet (85 gm) pineapple jelly
1 small sachet (10 gm) edible gelatin
500 gm vanilla ice cream
Juice of 1 lemon
5–6 glacé cherries to garnish (optional)

METHOD
1. Drain and reserve the pineapple syrup from the can.
2. Boil 1¼ cups water.
3. Add pineapple jelly granules to it and stir for 2 minutes until completely dissolved.
4. Then add 1¼ cup cold water. Stir and keep aside to cool.
5. Refrigerate for half an hour or till it sets partially.
6. In a separate non-stick pan, heat 1½ cups of the pineapple syrup.
7. Add the gelatin powder. Mix well and heat on a slow flame till the gelatin dissolves completely. Keep aside to cool. Then refrigerate.

8. When the jelly is partially set, combine it with the gelatin mix.
9. Chop 6 pineapple slices into cubes and keep aside. Reserve 3 slices for garnishing.
10. In a large bowl, break up the vanilla ice cream.
11. Add lemon juice and the jelly–gelatin mix.
12. Beat with a hand blender till the mix is of a smooth consistency.
13. Combine the pineapple cubes and mix well.
14. Set in a serving bowl and refrigerate for 4–5 hours.
15. When set, garnish with pineapple slices and some cherries.
16. Serve cold.

SHELF LIFE: Keep refrigerated and consume within 24 hours.

VALUE PER SERVING (¾ CUP)

Calories	197 kcal
Protein	4 gm
Fat	7 gm
Carbohydrates	31 gm
Fibre	0 gm
Calcium	94 mg
Iron	0 mg

Semolina and Dry Fruit Sheera

A light and quick Indian dessert enriched with dry fruits.

MAKES: 3 cups
SERVING SIZE: ½ cup

PREPARATION TIME: 5 mins
COOKING TIME: 30 mins

INGREDIENTS
½ cup fine semolina
1 cup toned milk
¾ cup granulated sugar
3 tbsp almonds, chopped finely
3 tbsp cashew nuts, chopped finely
2 tbsp brown raisins, chopped finely
2 pinches saffron strands
2 tbsp toned milk
2 tbsp *ghee*

METHOD
1. Soak the saffron strands in 2 tbsp hot milk and keep aside.
2. Heat ½ tsp ghee in a wok. Roast the cashews, almonds and semolina till the semolina is light brown in colour.
3. Meanwhile, boil 1 cup milk with ½ cup water in another pan. Stir in the boiled milk with the roasted semolina.

4. After 2 minutes, add the raisins and sugar. Cook for 5 minutes till the *sheera* reaches a thick paste-like consistency.
5. Add the saffron strands and milk to the above mix. Mix well and remove from flame.

SHELF LIFE: Keep refrigerated and consume within 24 hours.

VALUE PER SERVING (½ CUP)	
Calories	235 kcal
Protein	4 gm
Fat	9 gm
Carbohydrates	35 gm
Fibre	0 gm
Calcium	68 mg
Iron	1 mg

Walnut Fudge

A gooey dessert made from walnuts and desiccated coconut.

MAKES: 30 pieces
SERVING SIZE: 1 piece

PREPARATION TIME: 5 mins
COOKING TIME: 20 mins

INGREDIENTS
2¼ cups (200 gm) walnuts, chopped finely
1 tin (400 gm) condensed milk
1½ cups (100 gm) desiccated coconut (fresh and pure white in colour)
1½ tbsp cocoa powder
3–4 drops vanilla essence
1 tbsp melted butter

METHOD
1. Heat the melted butter in a pan.
2. Add condensed milk. On a medium flame, keep stirring the mixture so that it doesn't stick or get burnt at the bottom.
3. Cook for about 12 minutes till it thickens.
4. Add cocoa powder and chopped walnuts.
5. Combine ¾ cup desiccated coconut. Mix well.
6. The mixture will start turning sticky now, so keep stirring continuously for 2 minutes.
7. Add vanilla essence and cook for another minute. When the mixture stops sticking to the bottom, turn off the flame.

8. Immediately transfer the chocolaty mix onto a wide plate.
9. Grease your palms with a little butter.
10. While the mix is still hot, take 1 heaped tablespoon of it and roll into a small ball. Flatten a little and roll into the remaining desiccated coconut.
11. Repeat for the remaining mix to make another 29 balls.
12. No refrigeration required for 24 hours.

TIP: Make sure that the desiccated coconut is fresh and white in colour; refrigerate it to maintain its freshness and colour.

VALUE PER SERVING (1 PIECE)

Calories	111 kcal
Protein	2 gm
Fat	7 gm
Carbohydrates	9 gm
Fibre	1 gm
Calcium	7 mg
Iron	0 mg

Basic Recipes

Basic Wraps/Rotis for the Rolls

Use these rotis or wraps as a base for all the rolls.

MAKES: 12

INGREDIENTS
1 cup wholewheat flour
1 cup all-purpose flour
1 tsp oil (to add to dough)
6 tsp oil (for roasting the wraps)

METHOD
1. Combine the wholewheat flour, all-purpose flour, ¾ cup water and 1 tsp oil and knead into a soft and pliable dough.
2. Cover the dough with a wet muslin cloth and keep aside for 10 minutes.
3. Now divide the dough into twelve equal portions.
4. Roll out the portions with a rolling pin, with each portion measuring 5 inches in diameter.
5. Heat a *tava* and cook each wrap on both sides using ½ tsp oil for each.

Curd Dip

A creamy and flavourful dip which can be used with a variety of dishes.

MAKES: 1 cup
PREPARATION TIME: 5 mins

INGREDIENTS
8 tbsp thick fresh curd
4 tbsp fresh cream
1 tbsp cheese, grated
½ tbsp garlic, grated
3 tbsp lettuce, chopped finely
Salt and black pepper powder as per taste

METHOD
1. Combine all the ingredients in a bowl. Mix well.
2. Refrigerate and serve cold.

Flavoured/Plain Paneer

High-protein cottage cheese which can also be flavoured with Italian herbs.

MAKES: 125 gm
PREPARATION TIME: 5 mins
COOKING TIME: 15 mins

INGREDIENTS
1 litre toned milk
Juice of 1 lemon

ADDITIONAL INGREDIENTS FOR FLAVOURED PANEER:
1 tbsp mixed dried herbs (oregano, basil, paprika)

METHOD
TO MAKE PLAIN PANEER:
1. Bring the milk to a boil and turn off the flame.
2. Immediately add the lemon juice and stir until the milk curdles.
3. Strain through a muslin cloth, making sure all the liquid or whey is removed. What remains in the cloth is paneer.
4. Set the paneer to form in a firm disc shape by covering in a muslin cloth and placing a heavy weight over it.

TO MAKE FLAVOURED PANEER:
1. Add the dried herbs to the milk before heating and then continue with the first step above.

Ginger–Green Chilli Paste

Spicy paste made using green chillies and ginger.

MAKES: 1 tbsp
PREPARATION TIME: 5 mins

INGREDIENTS
6 green chillies
1-inch piece of ginger
5 drops of lemon juice
A pinch of salt

METHOD
1. Chop the ginger and green chillies coarsely.
2. Grind in a mixer along with salt and lemon juice.

Salsa Sauce

Tangy tomato salsa sauce with a zing of Mexican herbs.

MAKES: ½ cup
PREPARATION TIME: 5 mins
COOKING TIME: 8–10 mins

INGREDIENTS

1 large, fully ripe tomato, chopped finely
1 medium onion, chopped finely
1 tbsp ginger–green chilli paste (see recipe on p. 238)
1 tsp garlic paste
2 tbsp fresh basil leaves, chopped finely
1 tbsp dried herbs (Mexican seasoning)
1 tsp dried oregano
2 tsp olive oil
Salt as per taste

METHOD

1. Heat the olive oil. Sauté the ginger–green chilli paste and garlic paste.
2. Add onions and sauté till translucent.
3. Add tomato and salt as per taste; sauté for a minute.
4. Mash this mixture slightly with the back of a spoon.
5. Add basil leaves and sauté for half a minute.
6. Add oregano and Mexican seasoning.
7. Add 1 cup water and cook for 3–4 minutes. Turn off the flame and keep aside.

References

1. Mahan, L.K. and Sylvia Escott-Stump. 2000. *Krause's Food, Nutrition, & Diet Therapy*, pp. 242, 257. Philadelphia: W.B. Saunders.

2. Food Safety News. 2012. 'Tests Show Widespread Milk Adulteration in India'. Foodsafetynews.com, 11 January. Retrieved from http://www.foodsafetynews.com/2012/01/tests-show-widespread-milk-adulteration-in-india/#.VkGWe9IrLIU

3. Bush, S. 2015. 'Good Cholesterol in Hard-Boiled Eggs'. Livestrong.com, 22 June. Retrieved from http://www.livestrong.com/article/277221-good-cholesterol-in-hard-boiled-eggs/

4. WebMD. 2013. '7 Brain Foods for Kids'. Retrieved from http://www.webmd.com/add-adhd/childhood-adhd/features/brain-foods-kids?page=2

5. Toffelmire, Amy. 1996. 'Nutritional Benefits of Nuts', Canada.com. Retrieved from http://bodyandhealth.canada.com/channel_section_details.asp?text_id=4712&channel_id=9&relation_id=26047

6. Nuts for Life. 2012. 'Nuts and the Big Fat Myth: The Positive Role for Nuts in Weight Management'. The Nut Report 2012. Retrieved from http://www.walnut.net.au/

Resources/Documents/Research%20Programs/The-Nut-Report-Big-Fat-Myth-Oct2012.pdfhttp://www.walnut.net.au/Resources/Documents/Research%20Programs/The-Nut-Report-Big-Fat-Myth-Oct2012.pdf

7. Facts About Strawberries. 2009. 'Reasons to Eat Strawberries and Raspberries'. Retrieved from http://factsaboutstrawberries.blogspot.in/2009/11/reasons-to-eat-strawberries-and.html

8. Koathes, Stephanie. 2015. '7 Surprising Health Benefits of Bananas'. Loop, 12 August. Retrieved from http://www.loopt.com/content/7-surprising-health-benefits-bananas

9. Paul, Maya W. and Lawrence Robinson. 2015. 'Nutrition for Children and Teens'. Retrieved from http://www.helpguide.org/articles/healthy-eating/nutrition-for-children-and-teens.htm

10. Blaylock, Russell. 1996. *Excitotoxins: The Taste that Kills*. Albuquerque, NM: Health Press.

11. Smith, Lendon H. 1982. *Feed Your Kids Right*. Sydney: Random House Australia.

12. Nieburg, Oliver. 2015. 'Hershey's Milk Chocolate and Kisses to Go Non-GM'. Confectionerynews.com, 23 February. Retrieved from http://www.confectionerynews.com/Ingredients/Hershey-in-non-GMO-and-no-high-fructose-corn-syrup-pledge

13. Arnold, L. Eugene, Nicholas Lofthouse and Elizabeth Hurt. 2012. 'Artificial Food Colors and Attention-Deficit/Hyperactivity Symptoms: Conclusions to Dye For'. *Neurotherapeutics* 9 (3): 599–609. Retrieved from http://www.ncbi.nlm.nih.gov/pmc/articles/PMC3441937/

14. Schneider, Jens and Belinda Retief. 2015. '50 Toxic Food Additives You Should Not Feed Your Children', *4x4 wellness*, 17 March. Retrieved from http://www.4x4diet.com/50-toxic-food-additives-you-should-not-feed-your-children

15. Mahan, L.K., Sylvia Escott-Stump and Janice L. Raymond. 2012. *Krause's Food and the Nutrition Care Process*. Amsterdam, MO: Elsevier.

16. Fox News Insider. 2014. 'Dr. Oz Reveals the Hidden Dangers of Microwave Popcorn'. Fox and Friends, 28 April. Retrieved from http://insider.foxnews.com/2014/04/28/dr-oz-reveals-hidden-dangers-microwave-popcorn

17. Pandey, Vineeta. 2010. 'Mumbai Number Two on Child Obesity List: Study', *DNA*, 13 November. Retrieved from http://www.dnaindia.com/mumbai/report-mumbai-number-two-on-child-obesity-list-study-1465897

18. National Sleep Foundation. 1990–2015. 'Teens and Sleep'. Retrieved from http://sleepfoundation.org/sleep-topics/teens-and-sleep

19. Shute, Nancy. 2015. 'Sleeping Near a Smartphone Can Disturb a Child's Rest'. www.npr.org, 5 January. Retrieved from http://www.npr.org/sections/health-shots/2015/01/05/375121373/sleeping-near-a-smartphone-can-disturb-a-childs-rest

20. Berenjy, Shila and Parichehr Hanachi. 2008. 'Relation of Obesity and Menarche Age among Adolescent Students'. *Journal of Family and Reproductive Health* 2 (4): 173–77.

21. Pippig, Uta. 2006. 'Benefits of Exercise for Children: Get Up and Go!' TakeTheMagicStep.com. Retrieved from http://www.takethemagicstep.com/coaching/families/training-exercise/benefits-of-exercise-for-children/

22. Mahan et al., *Krause's Food and the Nutrition Care Process*.

23. Chumari, Alvin. 2015. 'How Smartphone and Tablet Overuse Can Harm Your Child's Health', HealthXchange.com.sg, 13 January. Retrieved from https://sg.news.yahoo.com/smartphone-tablet-overuse-harm-child-143240034.html

24. iKeepSafe.org. 'No Screen Time Before Bed'. Retrieved from http://ikeepsafe.org/be-a-pro/balance/no-screen-time-before-bed/

25. Greatist. 2014. 'Don't Have A Cow! Here's How To Pick The Best Milk For You', Forbes.com, 11 February. Retrieved from http://www.forbes.com/sites/greatist/2014/02/11/cows-milk-benefits-comparison/

26. Sanghvi, Roshni. 2012. 'Myths of Multigrain'. *Times of India*, The Crest Edition, 21 July 2012. Retrieved from http://www.timescrest.com/life/myths-of-multigrain-8387

27. Mahan and Escott-Stump, *Krause's Food, Nutrition, & Diet Therapy.*

28. Ibid.

29. National Institute of Nutrition, Indian Council of Medical Research. 2010. *Nutrient Requirements and Recommended Dietary Allowances for Indians*, pp. 174–75. Hyderabad: National Institute of Nutrition. Retrieved from http://icmr.nic.in/final/RDA-2010.pdf

30. Mahan and Escott-Stump, *Krause's Food, Nutrition, & Diet Therapy.*

31. Hendrick, B. 2010. 'Hookahs Safer than Cigarettes? A Pipe Dream'. WebMD Health News, 10 May. Retrieved from http://www.webmd.com/smoking-cessation/news/20100510/hookahs-safer-than-cigarettes-thats-a-pipe-dream

32. Burgess, Patrice and Kirtly Jones. 2014. 'Polycystic Ovary Syndrome (PCOS) — Topic Overview'. WebMD, 26 March 2014. Retrieved from http://www.webmd.com/women/tc/polycystic-ovary-syndrome-pcos-topic-overview#BM_Topic Overview

33. Balaji, Swetha, Chioma Amadi, Satish Prasad, Jyoti Bala Kasav, Vandana Upadhyay, Awnish K. Singh, Krishna Mohan Surapaneni and Ashish Joshi. 2015. 'Urban Rural Comparisons of Polycystic Ovary Syndrome Burden among Adolescent Girls in a Hospital Setting in India'. *Biomed Research International* 2015. Retrieved from http://www.ncbi.nlm.nih.gov/pmc/articles/PMC4299689/

34. Schulte-Hillen, Sophie. 2013. 'Can Food Cause Acne?' *Doctor Oz*, 30 January 2013. Retrieved from http://www.doctoroz.com/article/can-food-cause-acne

35. Mahan and Escott-Stump, *Krause's Food, Nutrition, & Diet Therapy*.

36. Ibid., p. 263.

37. National Institute of Nutrition, *Nutrient Requirements and Recommended Dietary Allowances for Indians*.

38. Umesh Kapil, G.T. 2011. 'Zinc Deficiency among Adolescents in Delhi'. *Indian Pediatrics* 48 (12): 981–82.

39. Mahan and Escott-Stump, *Krause's Food, Nutrition, & Diet Therapy*, p. 263

40. Lalonde, B. 2015. 'Vitamin D Deficiency & Skin Problems'. Livestrong.com, 4 May. Retrieved from http://www.livestrong.com/article/494425-vitamin-d-deficiency-skin-problems/

41. Mann, D. 2010. 'Guidelines Call for Increase in Vitamin D'. WebMD.com, 30 November. Retrieved from http://www.webmd.com/diet/20101129/guidelines-increase-vitamin-d

Acknowledgements

Every creation or organization is a product of teamwork. Proudly presenting my team who has really worked hard in bringing about this book. A huge thanks is due to you!

Anjali Kanodia, who has been a constant support all through my career. This book wouldn't have happened if not for her valuable contributions.

Priyanka Agarwal, my daughter, the perfectionist whose insights have played a huge role in shaping this book.

Vaishali and Vishakha, the twins, who are amazing with their innovative ideas and have helped me through various recipe trials and retrials.

Shwetal, for her research work.

Alka Saigal, for opening her beautiful Lonavala home to us so we could unplug and focus.

Adity Killa and Hetal Bhatkully for coming forward to do recipe trials.

Lastly, my staff, Kamla and Ravindra, for the preparation and cleaning after the recipe trials.

A Note on the Author

Diet guru and fitness expert Suman Agarwal is the force behind the action at Selfcare, a nutrition clinic that has led thousands of people including Bollywood celebs and industrial honchos to weight loss and good health through custom-designed diets. She follows a simple philosophy: Banish the boring. She contributes regularly to publications like *DNA*, *Femina*, *Beauty* and *Salon*, and has been featured in *Vogue*, *Bombay Times*, *Asian Age*, *Mid Day* and *Hindustan Times*, among others. Her previous book, *Unjunked*, received much critical acclaim.